## PAM GEMS

Amongst many other plays, Pam Gems is the author of *Dusa, Fish, Stas and Vi* (Hampstead and West End), *Queen Christina* (RSC), *Piaf* (RSC, West End and Broadway), *Camille* (RSC and West End), *The Blue Angel* (RSC) and *Deborah's Daughter* (Library Theatre, Manchester). She has produced versions of Chekhov's *Uncle Vanya* and *The Cherry Orchard*, as well as *The Seagull*, and of Ibsen's *A Doll's House* and *Ghosts*. She has also written two novels, *Mrs Frampton* and *Bon Voyage, Mrs Frampton*.

PAM GEMS

# STANLEY

NICK HERN BOOKS
London

**A Nick Hern Book**

*Stanley* first published in Great Britain as a paperback original in 1996 by Nick Hern Books, 14 Larden Road, London W3 7ST

Reprinted 1997

ISBN 1 85459 254 8

*Stanley* was first staged by the Royal National Theatre at the Cottesloe on 1 February 1996. First preview was 24 January. The cast was as follows:

| | |
|---|---|
| HILDA | Deborah Findlay |
| STANLEY | Antony Sher |
| HENRY | Pip Torrens |
| GWEN | Nicola King |
| PATRICIA | Anna Chancellor |
| AUGUSTUS | David Collings |
| DOROTHY | Selina Cadell |
| DUDLEY | Richard Howard |
| ELSIE | Stephanie Jacob |
| MRS CARLINE | Avril Elgar |
| BRIAN | Nicholas Deigman/ |
| | Daniel Forster-Smith |
| TIM | Robbie Morton/ |
| | Robert Smythson |

Other parts played by members of the Company

Pianist/keyboards                Walter Fabeck

*Director* John Caird
*Designer* Tim Hatley
*Lighting* Peter Mumford
*Music* J.S. Bach, *arranged by* Ilona Sekacz
*Company Voice Work* Patsy Rodenburg
*Dialect Coach* Jeannette Nelson
*Sound* Freya Edwards

## Characters

STANLEY
HILDA
PATRICIA
DOROTHY
GWEN
HENRY
AUGUSTUS
DUDLEY

ELSIE
MRS CARLINE

MODDOM
BETTY
NURSE

## Promenade

WORKMAN
MRS. BELLAMY
VICAR
TIM – BOY
BRIAN – BOY
SUMMERS – JOURNALIST
COLONEL
COLONEL'S WIFE

**Act One, Scene One**

STANLEY SPENCER's *studio.* STANLEY *is squaring up a canvas. He jumps down, winds up a gramophone, which plays Bach, returns to the canvas.*

HILDA *enters.*

HILDA. Sorry.

*She is eating out of a tin, gives him a bite. Then crosses, sits on a stool, drops the man's jacket from her shoulders and resumes a pose.* STANLEY *leaves what he is doing, picks up a pad and resumes sketching her. As the Bach ends* HILDA *leans over and stops the gramophone.* STANLEY *goes on humming.*

HILDA. Then there's the light. No comparison. (STANLEY *does not reply or acknowledge her.*) The moment you're south of Lyons everything comes alive! (*No response. He scratches away, glancing at her.*) Don't you *want* to see Italy? Verona? Vicenza?

STANLEY (*absorbed*). Nothing to do with place.

HILDA. You say paint is the most convincing medium –

STANLEY. Anybody can see, ducky. If painting's to be just about looking then it's no more important than my shirt button.

HILDA. What else is it about? Of course it's about looking, what else is there?

*He throws down the sketchbook and springs, fetching up before her, waving the pencil in her face.*

STANLEY. What else is there! Love!

*Light change.* HILDA *on her stomach on the floor,* STANLEY *walking about in full flow.*

STANLEY. What is it that sets out the identity of everything
we know . . . rips away meaninglessness? Love . . . passion.
That's what we're here for . . . that's our job. To reveal the
nature of the world. Through love. Look. (*He fans through
canvases, hauls out an unfinished work, slams it on an
easel.*)

(*Points.*) Christ! I've got Him kneeling in a deep pit of
madder soil . . . His whole body stretched between heaven
and earth . . . over there are supplicants flopping
and crumpling up in ecstasy, then I've done Him again . . .
here . . . His body flung onto the grass, He's holding the
grass in rapture – remember when you were small and the
blades of grass seemed big . . . He's big and small at the
same time, d'you see?

HILDA. I remember walking through bracken when the fronds
were over my head.

STANLEY. Paint it! You get blind alleys of course, but so long
as the search is a loving search . . .

*He falters. And stands, across from her, without expression.
And then he begins to shake gently.* HILDA *is on her feet
at once. She enfolds him, and rocks him like a child in her
arms. Then they kiss gently. She gazes at him tenderly, to
see if he is all right. He looks away.*

HILDA (*strokes his hair*). What was it like?

*He looks at her, already wary. She shakes him slightly. He
pulls away from her, goes back to his drawing. Silence as
he draws.*

STANLEY (*at last*). One thing I do remember.

*But he does not go on. She waits.*

HILDA. What?

STANLEY (*dismissive*). Ohh . . . just the way the men who
were mustering to go to France for the first time . . . (*He
draws obsessively.*) . . . always the same . . . 'Come on, lads,
what are we waiting for – we'll show 'em!' (*He looks up at
her, bends to the drawing.*) The wounded . . . those on the
way back . . . they never said a word. No, don't move.

(*Stands back.*) I think I'll do a row of fuzz bushes round this bit . . . a ring of fire . . .

*He draws.* HILDA *looks beautiful in the light. He contemplates her.*

STANLEY (*shudders*). Urgh, that hospital was cold!

HILDA (*puzzled*). Hospital?

STANLEY. Before the war it was a lunatic asylum . . . Kench, our Sergeant-Major, had been Head Nurse there, before that in the Marines. God, he was terrifying. And his dog.

HILDA (*laughs*). The Hound of the Baskervilles?

STANLEY. Oh much worse. An airedale. Even Matron was afraid of that dog and she made Queen Mary look like a frightened little wisp. Turn your head, I want the back of your neck.

(*Draws.*) The Holy Trinity. Seven foot sergeant, red-eyed dog – and Deborah.

HILDA. The Matron?

STANLEY. No, one of the male loonies – (*As* HILDA *makes to enquire.*) – God knows, somebody's idea of a joke I suppose.

HILDA. Why, was he hideous?

STANLEY. No. Ordinary enough. Most of the time he just walked about with his eyes down. Bit sinister, though – for example, you couldn't leave knives out. Still, I envied Deborah.

HILDA. Why?!

STANLEY. He never even knew there was a war on. Cut off from his soul, d'you see? (*He draws.*)

HILDA. What WAS it like? (*She waits, watching for signs of distress. His face is expressionless, then suddenly there is a rictus of a grimace, frightening.*)

STANLEY. I . . . I wasn't able to . . . just one lorry after another. Bodies. People – pieces of people. Arms . . . legs . . . all lovingly made. Somebody had to bury them.

HILDA. You worked in a hospital? Stanley, I thought you were infantry.

STANLEY. I transferred. Volunteered for active duty in Macedonia.

HILDA. Oh I see, you WANTED to get killed!

STANLEY. The hills were so beautiful I didn't want to be sent behind the lines. No. You do things sometimes . . . I expect it's being short, you have to prove yourself. Men aren't brave, you know. They try to be. I don't want to see all that again. Friends – people you sleep next to in the trench turned into convolvulus – entrails hanging on the wire. Or looking ordinary, only dead. Clearing out their belongings – one lad had a snap of his pet pig.

HILDA. What did you do with it?

STANLEY. Sent it home to his mother.

HILDA *stifles a laugh.* STANLEY *glares at her then laughs, becoming hysterical, drawing in whooping breaths and shrieking.* HILDA *holds him.*

HILDA. It's all right . . . it's all right . . . (*She rocks him back and forth till he subsides.*) Better out than in.

STANLEY. That could have a dirty meaning, you know. (*He touches her auburn hair.*) You make me think of night. I remember once – I was sitting in the snow behind the lines . . . they started to move us up, and . . . I don't know what happened, but . . . trying to march in the ruts and . . . somebody moaning . . . I can't bear any more of this, I thought, and all of a sudden it was as if the stars turned warm. As if the snow had little flames, licking up round me, so I felt . . . it's all right . . . everything is as it should be! . . .

HILDA. Oh my dear . . . in all that – !

STANLEY. I know. I was surrounded by the most horrible sights yet it was as if I was in a great big church of the world . . . like lights streaming down from clerestory windows . . . on me . . . I was in the middle of it . . . I was it. (*He searches for the right word.*) I felt . . . unselfish. It was lovely. I had *tried* to be like the saints, but it's very hard

to believe in a life of sacrifice when the pus is shooting up in
your eyes. If you could just hang on to it . . . everything
clear! Carry that blinding moment of worship inside you
like the ark of the covenant. Perhaps that's it. Perhaps if
I could hang on to moments like that . . . perhaps by being
unselfish . . . Do you think that's it? Is that how to get to a
pure imagination . . . to beauty? Through virtue? Is that the
only way?

HILDA. I don't know, Stanley.

STANLEY. Maybe when I meet my Maker I'll ask Him . . . in
a humble way of course, to take into consideration all the
men I've cleaned and all the floors I've scrubbed.

HILDA. And your pictures!

STANLEY. Oh yes! I'd like to think He'd like a few of them
around – after all, they're His creation . . . via me – (*Touches
her face.*) I'm so grateful. To be alive. Guilty. (*Recovers.*)
I can't believe it. I couldn't have married anyone else.
The first time I saw you in that jacket with the grey braid
I thought – ah, there she is. You touched my arm, it was so
mysterious. And when you took my arm in a more ordinary
way it was even more profound.

HILDA. You came to dinner. In Hampstead.

STANLEY. And you served the soup and looked at everyone
except me. I wanted to burst out laughing!

HILDA. That made you know? That I liked you?

STANLEY. Plus the fact you left your bedroom door open so
I could see the top of your leg when you were putting on
your stocking . . . oooooh! (*He crosses to the large canvas,
squares up.*) I couldn't believe my luck. It was getting to
the stage where I had to meet somebody . . . all my lovely
Stanley-feelings were being . . . I mean, if I hadn't met you
I might have had to settle for 'Hullo, our Stan, been at the old
painting again?' (HILDA *laughs.*) I shall put you up here . . .
sitting . . . then I'll do you again over here sniffing a daisy,
I'll do another group rising up out of their tombs and feeling
all lazy and cheerful and happy to be alive, and not in a
hurry to move off. I want the feeling to be like Cookham . . .

sort of Ascot, Sunday afternoon, Boulter's Lock, in-the-body sort of life, but seen spiritually.

HILDA. It's going to be wonderful.

STANLEY. I tell you something. They won't think I'm simple when I put this up.

HILDA. They don't think you're simple.

STANLEY. Oh no?!

HILDA. They only tease you because – (*She turns away from his furious face in order to suppress her laughter.*) Stan! You're brilliant!... everyone knows that. (*She puts an arm on his shoulder.*) A great artist's eye is never naive. (*They contemplate the canvas together.*)

STANLEY. I miss it though.

HILDA. What?

STANLEY. How it was . . . before sex. Just that clear child's eye. I miss that.

HILDA (*puts an arm about his waist*). We wouldn't have this, though. (*He turns to her.*)

STANLEY. No. We wouldn't. (*They embrace tenderly.*) It's perfect, isn't it? (*She nods. They kiss deeply.*)

**Act One Scene Two**

*A London studio. Messy and paint-splashed. An old trestle table is loaded with drink. There are several old painty chairs, an easy chair, broken, a divan, a large, country-house style pouffe with the stuffing hanging out, and a good oak elbow chair. Present are HENRY, GWEN, HILDA, STANLEY and DUDLEY. DUDLEY, older, sits in the elbow chair.*

HENRY (*calls from the drinks table*). It was Matisse. He learned it from Manet.

GWEN. What?

HILDA. That black is a colour.

GWEN. You mean, not absence of colour? Augustus!

AUGUSTUS JOHN, *in cloak and wide awake, enters, with* DOROTHY HEPWORTH *and* PATRICIA PREECE *on his arms.*

HENRY. The man himself!

AUGUSTUS. Of course it's a colour, real tin-opener when you want it – right, Cookham?

STANLEY *rears up from the divan, blinks.*

AUGUSTUS (*introducing his companions*). Bookends!

GWEN. Augustus don't be filthy.

AUGUSTUS. Miss Hepworth . . . Miss Preece – right, Gwen, what's it to be – grub or you?

PATRICIA. He's already exposed himself to half Chelsea. (*She looks round coolly as* DOROTHY *talks to* HENRY, *decides on* DUDLEY *to talk to.*) I believe you're a patron of the arts. Patricia Preece.

GWEN (*calls*). Dudley – Augustus is going to paint T.E. Lawrence! (*She gets food for* AUGUSTUS.)

STANLEY, *supine on the divan, rears up.*

STANLEY. He's a fraud!

HENRY. Who?

HILDA. Lawrence of Arabia.

AUGUSTUS. He is not.

STANLEY. Yes he is. (*To* DOROTHY, *standing close by.*) Isn't he!

DOROTHY. Does rather back into the limelight, I'd say.

AUGUSTUS (*to* DOROTHY, *pugnacious*). Ever met him?

*She shakes her head. He wheels on* STANLEY.

Know him?

STANLEY. Nope.

AUGUSTUS (*hauling* STANLEY *up by his tie*). Then shut your mouth.

STANLEY *rushes at* AUGUSTUS, *brings him down. They grapple, rolling over and over. No-one takes the slightest notice except to move out of their way.* HENRY, HILDA, GWEN *and* DOROTHY *are having an argument.*

HENRY. No, no, no, no, no, no . . . it's over!

DUDLEY. The Pre-Raphaelites the last twitch of the corpse?

HENRY. Absolutely. From now on, anything goes.

STANLEY *looks up from the scrap.*

STANLEY. No it doesn't.

HENRY. Shut up, Cookham, stick to your peasants.

STANLEY. What are you talking about, you paint people . . . you painted portraits!

HENRY. Sorry. I did *try* to make you look like Valentino.

AUGUSTUS. Enshrined for posterity, eh Stan? (*Laughs.*) Here's to figure painting! (*Claps* STANLEY *genially on the back, knocking him over.*)

STANLEY (*slightly dazed with drink and the blow*). I bow the knee . . . Giotto!

HENRY. Rubbish . . . Taxidermy! Realism's for embalmers. (*Fills a water glass with whisky; drinks.*) Here's to the radical!

GWEN. The Avant-Garde!

STANLEY Avant – ? And what, if you don't mind, is more radical than the real? (*Since* PATRICIA *is the closest, he addresses it to her.*)

PATRICIA (*dismissive*). What's real?

STANLEY. People. (*To* PATRICIA.). Aren't people real?

*But she merely shrugs, walks away.*

PATRICIA (*to* DOROTHY). Is he anybody?

STANLEY. Look at the Italians –

AUGUSTUS. The Dutch –

STANLEY. The early primitives –

HENRY (*points at* AUGUSTUS). Sentimental – (*Points at* STANLEY.) . . . and provincial!

STANLEY. If I'm provincial, so's Caravaggio!

DOROTHY. Yes, he painted ordinary people.

DUDLEY. Absolutely! Bravo, my boy.

HENRY. Hardly your grocers – ladies with round bottoms.

AUGUSTUS. Don't put him off those, do you the world of good, Cookham.

HILDA. Augustus, would you shut up, Stanley has a perfectly adequate bottom provided in his household by me.

STANLEY. I'm not impressed – (*A shout of laughter.*) No, I don't mean about – (*He flashes* HILDA *a black look.*)

HILDA. Oh dear . . . now I'm for it.

STANLEY (*to* HENRY). You and the bloody avant-garde . . . just use the word and you're bogus –

GWEN. Why?

STANLEY. It's showing off! Being outside, looking in, when you're in who cares about labels . . . all so frightened of being caught out . . . ooh, I mustn't be old hat, what's this kipper stuck on the wall, marvellous! – well it might be, but not when it's 'Avant-Garde' . . . just another way to frighten people off their own ecstasy, can't have that, might stop the production line, do you know the trouble with the human race?

HENRY. They talk too much.

STANLEY. A fatal and suicidal talent for adaptability . . . most of all to being less than human.

DUDLEY. Human? I think that got washed out at Ypres . . . on the Somme. Nowadays . . . nowadays . . . well, there's shopping.

PATRICIA. I'm rather fond of shopping. (*She smiles at* DOROTHY, *who pulls a wry face.*)

DUDLEY. Yes.

STANLEY. You can't just settle for things. Oh yes! I know . . .

'he's off again' . . . you'll pick up on anything that's ready-made hand-me-down.

AUGUSTUS (*getting sleepy*). Go on, Stan!

STANLEY. Vorticist . . . Surrealist . . . all this fashion for Idea – you think that's what it takes to fill a canvas? Fill space for the glory of God? To paint from Here . . . (*He bangs his chest.*) – it's the hardest, hardest thing . . . anybody can do it from the mind . . . but from the heart . . .

It took me a year to sort out The Apple Gatherers. I kept funking it.

PATRICIA. Did you say The Apple Gatherers?

STANLEY. Yes.

PATRICIA. Are you Stanley Spencer?

STANLEY. Yes.

PATRICIA. I thought your name was Cookham. (*She scowls at DOROTHY for not telling her.*)

STANLEY. It's where I live. I go on about it, it makes them laugh. I'm sorry for the lot of you!

GWEN. Me? Why?

STANLEY (*points at them*). Orphans! Bunged off to school from the cradle, what do you know about home? Ohh, home! Looking down from the nursery window like cherubim and seraphim, listening to Annie playing the viola after she'd put us to bed . . . Ma sewing under the lamp, Pa polishing his brass plate by the door . . . 'Professor of Music'! . . . Will trying a Bach partita, Gil sketching. . . (*He sniffs it all in.*) Oh, the feel of everything . . . wet ivy by the door, cold lino, the iron latch on the privy in winter – I spent hours in that privy watching woodlice, drove them all mad . . . and the smells! Our old dog coming in with a wet coat . . . barley soup . . . burnt feathers when you singed off a boiling fowl . . .

*The lights go down during the above. Everyone sleepy with drink. Silence. Then AUGUSTUS farts a long fart, exactly to the rhythm of 'The curfew tolls the knell of parting day.'*

DOROTHY (*after a beat*). 'The homeward shepherd –

HILDA. – wanders o'er the lea.'

*Laughter.* PATRICIA *rises, stretches. And scratches her pubes. She catches* STANLEY'*s eye.*

HENRY. Trouble with the minge, Preece?

PATRICIA (*gazing at* STANLEY *without expression*). Pube itch.

HILDA *struggles into her coat.* GWEN *and* HENRY *help* AUGUSTUS *out.* DOROTHY *waits by the door for* PATRICIA, *who contemplates* STANLEY. HILDA *and* DOROTHY *exit, talking together.*

PATRICIA. You're Stanley Spencer.

STANLEY. I am.

GWEN *enters.*

GWEN. Augustus has lost his teeth.

*She crawls round, searching.* STANLEY *looks up at* PATRICIA.

STANLEY. Well?

PATRICIA *surveys* STANLEY *coolly.*

PATRICIA. He's rather a delicious little thing.

GWEN. Now, now, Patricia. Ah . . . got 'em!

*She brandishes the teeth, rises. Goes.*

PATRICIA. Is she usually so motherly?

STANLEY. What?

PATRICIA. I've seen you before. In Cookham. Dorothy and I live in Moor Thatch, the cottage by the meadow.

DOROTHY (*at the door*). Peggy, are you coming?

PATRICIA. In a manner of speaking.

DOROTHY *disappears.* STANLEY *gets up.*

STANLEY. Nice woman, Miss Hepworth.

PATRICIA. She has a heart. If you like that sort of thing.

*She gazes at* STANLEY, *then goes. He prances, pleased with himself.*

## Act One Scene Three

STANLEY*'s bedroom. ELSIE, the buxom maid to the Spencers, strips off the dirty sheets. She sniffs at them; they are smelly.*

ELSIE. Phew! (*She remakes the bed with fresh sheets expertly, singing the hymn 'We Plough the Fields and Scatter'.*)

STANLEY, *entering, joins in.*

ELSIE. That you, Mr Spencer? Shan't be long.

STANLEY. No hurry. (*He watches with pleasure as she bends over the bed, showing her thighs. He moves in to help, pausing for a sniff as he passes her.*) Mmmm . . . carbolic! I'll do you in your pinny, Elsie. Under the tree.

ELSIE. Not tonight, you won't. I got a date with Clark Gable.

STANLEY. You don't like him better than me, do you?

ELSIE. It's that little 'tache I shouldn't wonder. There, you'll do.

*She leans, smooths the coverlet, picks up the dirty linen and plods off.* STANLEY *watches her appreciatively.*

STANLEY. Ooh I do love a head of hair under the armpits.

*He starts to undress, dropping his braces. Lights to low.* STANLEY, *in bed, lying against the pillows, is watching* HILDA *undress.*

STANLEY. It's so lovely sending my thoughts to you.

HILDA (*sits naked, brushing her hair*). I know.

STANLEY. It's like sending them home. You wing them out knowing they'll pair off and find pals. (*He watches her.*) It won't make any difference, will it?

HILDA *puts down her brush, rises and crosses, and gets into bed beside him.*

HILDA. Move over, of course it won't.

STANLEY. What will I have to do?

HILDA. Nothing. Just love both of us.

STANLEY. Think I can manage that.

*But he broods, frowning. She turns to him. He turns away
from her, on his side.*

HILDA. Ssssh. Nothing – nothing – nothing – will ever come
between us. How could it? We're too close. We're one.
We're married. One flesh. Us. You and me. It's sacred, and
we're sacred and you're adorable and I love every part of
you and it's wonderful . . . wonderful never to be shy . . . to
know and be known and be able to be completely open and
not have to worry . . . to be open, open, open. It means to be
well. Stanley – Stanley? Gone to sleep?

*He jumps on her.*

HILDA. Stan, no . . . be careful. We'd better not.

STANLEY. Why?

HILDA. It might hurt things.

STANLEY. No it won't.

*He rolls off her. Silence.*

HILDA. All right, then. If you're careful. (*But he does not
reply, merely watches her with a brooding stare.*) Be
careful! . . . that's all I meant. (*Still no response. So she
struggles back into her nightdress.*)

STANLEY. Oh yes. On it goes.

HILDA. But you –

*He lies back, regarding her as she turns, freeing her hair.*

STANLEY. I ask myself . . . 'Stan? Is Hilda Carline deserving
of your complete love and devotion?' And the answer is –
'no.' (*As she tries to speak he sits up, pointing.*) If the best
I had to offer fitted like a glove . . . if I knew I could make
you completely happy nothing would give me more joy than
to pursue that love. As it is . . .

HILDA. Stanley, what have you been up to?

STANLEY. I went to see the women. The posh pair. They
haven't got two pennies to rub together, so I took some logs
round and got their fire going.

HILDA. I wondered why you smelled of smoke. (*She climbs into bed again, snuggles up.*) Come on . . . (*He doesn't respond.*) I want you. Now. In. (*He turns his back on her. As she closes he moves away even further, almost falling out of bed.*) All right. Suit yourself. (*She turns down the lamp. Silence.*)

STANLEY. They were so baroque.

HILDA. What?

STANLEY. In the firelight. Their lovely forms. The two women.

HILDA. Oh.

STANLEY. I found it a mite disconcerting. She was wearing a sort of pink wrap . . .

HILDA. Patricia?

STANLEY. With tassels.

HILDA *whistles.*

One sleeve kept falling off her shoulder. It made me feel all glowing. (*He jerks away from her.*)

STANLEY. Stop it.

HILDA. I want you.

STANLEY. I don't know why you're always after me when I particularly don't want you. If you can be so obtuse when you're supposed to be closer than anyone in the whole world . . . in any case, it's obvious you think I only do big pictures to be self-important –

HILDA. No I don't –

*He jumps out of bed, looms over her.*

STANLEY. Big pictures, big head . . . that's what you meant. And saying I'm always talking about myself . . . it's my natural feeling of wanting to share everything . . . how can you say you like the hyacinths best, well we know what you think of the imaginary stuff now . . . I only did the shitty hyacinths because I was bored!

HILDA. Oh Stanley!

STANLEY. Now we get the truth of it –

HILDA. Is that what it's all about! Not Patricia Preece in her
shimmy . . . not the baby . . . oh, bliss!

STANLEY. How can you . . . it's comical! I don't understand
any of it, how it can be . . . how I can hate your ideas so
much and . . . well . . . love you –

HILDA. Sorry? Could you say that again? I didn't see your lips
move.

STANLEY (*starts to dress*). If there's one thing I despise in
human beings it's sarcasm. The refuge of the barren. If you
were as honest as I am – which you are not – you would
acknowledge that you hate my ideas as much as I hate yours.
But no. All you do is say 'Ooh, now I like that!'! I don't
know where I am. I've always felt so natural and alive with
you, I've never thought – Ah, I mustn't say this or that or
she won't understand, even though you often don't
understand, in fact, the way you looked at my big picture
blighted my desire to talk to you about painting at all!

*He takes out his small sketchpad, crosses to Moor Thatch,
where DOROTHY and PATRICIA are sitting together.
DOROTHY leaves and PATRICIA stretches out posing,
as STANLEY sketches her.*

HILDA. What's the matter?

PATRICIA. I feel a fool, talking about my work to you.

STANLEY. Can't Miss Hepworth take a job?

PATRICIA. She paints too!

STANLEY. Oh. Yes.

PATRICIA. And we don't sell. So, penniless, Q.E.D.

STANLEY (*busy drawing*). Q.E.D?

PATRICIA. It means –

STANLEY. I know what it means.

PATRICIA. What does it mean?

STANLEY *puts down his pencil, comes over to her.*

STANLEY. It doesn't mean that because I put my hand here, I don't respect you.

*She laughs, removes his hand from her groin. He smells his hand, closing his eyes in ecstasy. She chuckles, but watches him objectively.*

PATRICIA. Sometimes you're almost there. For an Englishman. Well, like the chimp at the typewriter trying for Shakespeare.

STANLEY, *furious, makes to go.*

STANLEY. You'll be sorry you said that.

PATRICIA. Why, what are you going to do to me?

STANLEY. You know what you are!

PATRICIA. I'm a lot of things. (*Calls after him.*) What are you?

STANLEY *goes.* DOROTHY *enters at once.*

PATRICIA. I suppose YOU were being discreet.

DOROTHY. No.

PATRICIA. What were you doing out there?

DOROTHY. Choosing a saucepan to hit you over the head with.

PATRICIA. What's the matter?

DOROTHY. Please, not the innocent child. I'm tired.

PATRICIA. Oh well, of course, you work All the time.

DOROTHY. One of us has to.

PATRICIA. I pay my way.

DOROTHY. No you don't.

PATRICIA. That is a vile thing to say.

DOROTHY. I'm not the one who's being vile.

PATRICIA *rears dangerously.*

If you have to misbehave I wish you wouldn't do it under this roof.

PATRICIA. Misbehave? Misbehave? Well . . . if my mis-
behaviour is so offensive to you why put up with it?

DOROTHY. Who else would?

PATRICIA. Oh I see – favours! Thank you. Thank you very
much. Has it escaped your notice that I have never had the
least trouble in attracting whosoever –

DOROTHY. Whomsoever –

PATRICIA. Whomsoever my heart desires?

DOROTHY. We weren't talking about attracting people.

PATRICIA. Weren't we? I thought we were.

DOROTHY. We were talking about keeping people.

PATRICIA (*slight pause*). As far as that goes, some of us
prefer to move on. Do remember that.

DOROTHY. I'm sure you will. Move on. When you find a
better billet. I know that.

PATRICIA. Oh . . . poor thing! I couldn't live with myself if
I were such a fool as you. You're a fool.

DOROTHY. Yes.

PATRICIA. Why put up with me!

DOROTHY *considers this seriously.*

DOROTHY. Who knows?

Perhaps it's –

I can't paint ALL the time. Most of the day, yes, especially
now I'm doing stuff for you to exhibit . . . (*As* PATRICIA
*makes to protest.*) . . . No, no, have what you need . . . still . . .
there are moments when one doesn't feel like work. The odd
instant.

PATRICIA. So I'm there to fall back on?

DOROTHY. Yes, in a way.

PATRICIA. As a fill-in?

DOROTHY. I suppose so . . . yes. And you do make me laugh,
of course.

PATRICIA. I WHAT?

*She begins to hurl things at* DOROTHY, *who dodges.*

DOROTHY. You did ask . . . ow! I'm doing you the courtesy of being truthful.

PATRICIA (*furious*). Why?! Honest people don't tell the truth – only Pigs!

*Running out of things to throw, she attacks* DOROTHY, *who falls, struggling to rise and contain* PATRICIA, *who strikes out at her.* DOROTHY *pulls herself up onto the sofa and grasps* PATRICIA, *pinning her arm. We get the impression this has happened before.*

DOROTHY. Stop it – stop it, Pixie . . . you're all right . . . I'm here . . . I'm here.

PATRICIA. Mean! Mean about presents, mean about money . . .

DOROTHY. I know.

PATRICIA. Me selfish? – what about last night? Four o'clock in the morning I get up to piddle – and you've put the light out! I was in the dark!

DOROTHY. So you said over breakfast. And over lunch.

PATRICIA. I could have been killed!

DOROTHY. I know. I'm a mean miser.

PATRICIA. Yes, you are.

DOROTHY. A foul fiend.

PATRICIA *leans back against* DOROTHY's *knees.*

DOROTHY. I won't do it again.

PATRICIA. Promise?

DOROTHY *leans down and kisses her gently.* PATRICIA *makes to nestle, looks round.* DOROTHY, *knowing what she wants, leans over and picks up a Teddy Bear, gives it to* PATRICIA. DOROTHY *goes on hugging* PATRICIA.

PATRICIA. After all, it was your idea, selling the paintings under my name.

DOROTHY. Absolutely – Peggy, it's fine.

PATRICIA. If I didn't have to do all the selling I could get down to more painting myself, instead of having to rush about all the time.

DOROTHY. I'm grateful.

PATRICIA. It's all very well, Hepworth. You just skulk around here doing what you want!

DOROTHY. It's your good nature, dearest. You naturally need to help people.

PATRICIA. I know. (*Leans up for a kiss.*) When I'm with you the maggots leave my head. I feel like Emperior Hirohito.

DOROTHY. What?

PATRICIA. When he came on the state visit . . . Maud told me . . . the king put an arm on his shoulder at breakfast, just being civil. Now the Emperor has English breakfast every day in memory of the ecstasy of it all . . . no-one was ever allowed to touch him before.

*She snuggles happily. Brief pause.*

DOROTHY. Darling . . .

PATRICIA. Mm?

DOROTHY. Don't flirt with Stanley Spencer.

PATRICIA. Only trying to please. He does have his uses.

DOROTHY. Such as?

PATRICIA. Dudley Tooth is his agent for one.

DOROTHY. Not fair to lead him on, though. Noblesse oblige, Pixie.

PATRICIA. Dreadful little oik. Gives me the horrors.

DOROTHY. So you won't sit for him again?

PATRICIA. Are you mad? You saw his sketches! He's only interested in malformation – he's drawn me all crooked!

**Act One Scene Four**

*The studio.* STANLEY *working, whistling.* HILDA *enters, with baby in pram.* STANLEY *leans down for a look.*

STANLEY. What are you going to call it?

HILDA. Shut up!

STANLEY. Oh, nice name. Is it supposed to look all squashed?

HILDA (*going*). And, where are my violets, the ones I picked this morning? I left them on the draining board. You didn't. Stan, you didn't take them round there.

STANLEY. Well-bred women like flowers . . . she wanted them for her room.

HILDA. Her? Which her? Who are you pinching flowers for, Stanley? The nice little one or the vicious one with the bony cheeks?

STANLEY (*painting rapidly*). I know what I should put here – a scold with evil glinting eyes looking down to make sure no-one enjoys themselves – especially the men!

HILDA. Good, then the women can have some fun!

*Debris is hurled at him. He yells, dodges, and falls off the trestle.*

*Over at* DOROTHY'*s,* PATRICIA *is on her stomach, reading.* DOROTHY *enters.*

DOROTHY. Peggy . . . you're very quiet, what are you doing?

PATRICIA. Reading!

DOROTHY. Reading?!

PATRICIA. Don't be so insulting. I read a lot.

DOROTHY. When?

PATRICIA. Shut up. This happens to be extremely deep, I'm concentrating.

DOROTHY (*taking off her hat*). What is it?

PATRICIA. A book!

DOROTHY. Oh, I thought it was a duck-billed platypus.

PATRICIA *gives a little snicker of laughter.*

PATRICIA. There – you see? I do have a sense of humour.

DOROTHY. Who says not?

PATRICIA. That fish-eyed Hilda Spencer. She told Augustus John that I was a Narcissist.

DOROTHY. Hilda?

PATRICIA. And you know what he said? It's sexual.

DOROTHY. Well he would.

PATRICIA. Anyway I asked Frankie Bacon and he said to see the chap in Hampstead.

DOROTHY. What chap?

PATRICIA. Glasses – beard – weird first name –

DOROTHY. Sigmund?

PATRICIA. Possibly.

DOROTHY. Not Dr. Freud?

PATRICIA. That's the chappie. So I rang Maynard and Lydia for the address, and took a cab.

DOROTHY *winces at the expense.*

DOROTHY. Not all the way?

PATRICIA. I could have been seriously ill! D'you know, when I got there, every door wide open . . . in the rain! Claustrophobia.

DOROTHY. You?

PATRICIA. Him. The Herr Doktor.

*This baffles* DOROTHY.

DOROTHY (*taking the book*). What did he say?

PATRICIA. Gave me that. I said I'd send on a cheque.

DOROTHY (*nods, gives back the book*). Didn't offer to analyse you then?

PATRICIA. I'm not a lunatic, thank you! Look, d'you mind shutting up, this happens to be extremely deep.

DOROTHY. What does it say?

PATRICIA *frowns, looking for the place.*

PATRICIA. Here we are. 'Narcissism. Point One. Venomous rages.' Well that's hardly surprising, Hilda Spencer would try the patience of Saint Agnes.

DOROTHY. Why, what's she done?

PATRICIA. Nothing, she never does. Just sits about being natural – it's unnerving. No wonder he's sick of her.

DOROTHY. Is he – sick of her?

PATRICIA. I didn't say that.

DOROTHY, *puzzled, shakes her head, trying to make sense of this. She gives up.*

DOROTHY. Go on about Narcissism.

PATRICIA (*reads*). 'Point Two. Manipulating Others.'

DOROTHY. That's two you've won.

PATRICIA *tosses the book over the back of the sofa.*

PATRICIA. The rest is just medical mumbo-jumbo – and they're totally wrong about no sense of humour. However . . .

*She gets up, prowls thoughtfully, picking up the book and clutching it to her.*

PATRICIA. Give Spencer her due, she's absolutely on the nail for once. I AM a narcissist.

DOROTHY. You are?

PATRICIA. Oh yes. No question about it.

DOROTHY. How exactly do you mean?

PATRICIA. Oh God, Dodsy, you are a great block of wood and no nails sometimes – honestly! (*She sighs patiently at* DOROTHY*'s stupidity.*) Narcissus liked to gaze in pools to see his own reflection because he was so Beautiful!

DOROTHY *laughs apart – changing to puzzlement as* PATRICIA *begins to strip off.*

DOROTHY. What are you doing?

PATRICIA. Stanley's coming.

DOROTHY. When?

PATRICIA. Now.

DOROTHY. Why?

PATRICIA. To paint me.

DOROTHY. You?

PATRICIA. Yes.

DOROTHY. Here?

PATRICIA (*lying back naked*). In the buff.

STANLEY, *working, glares across at* HILDA, *feeding the baby.*

STANLEY. I can't work with her in here.

HILDA. I'm feeding!

*He watches jealously, then jumps down, grabs a sketch pad and begins to sketch them.*

STANLEY (*working absolutely furiously*). How am I supposed to work? (*As* HILDA *bends over the baby, whispering softly to her.*) I need you! (*She takes no notice.*) I need you vibrant, full of life . . . sort of challenging me so I never quite know where I am. What I don't want is you tired . . . (*She looks up.*) . . . with that look on your face. If I'm to work I have to feel right, and people have to see to it that I'm all right and not feeling riled or fed up or in a brooding sort of way . . . know what I mean, ducky?

HILDA *looks up from the baby, only half-listening.* STANLEY *throws down his charcoal, crosses to* PATRICIA.

STANLEY. No, keep still.

PATRICIA *is lying naked.* STANLEY *is drawing her.*

PATRICIA. Oh you are a bore. I don't really care for being looked at, you know.

STANLEY (*stops drawing.*) All right. (*Comes close.*) I'll do it when you aren't looking.

PATRICIA. Fool.

STANLEY (*grabs her shoe, kisses it.*) I'll buy you a red pair.

PATRICIA. I'd prefer emeralds.

STANLEY. Sorry?

PATRICIA. A decent bracelet, or . . . so long as it isn't amethysts or anything common.

STANLEY (*thinking that she is joking*). Oh well, absolutely, my lady. How about diamonds – sapphires . . . they do?

PATRICIA. If you like.

*He gazes up at her like a rabbit in headlights.*

STANLEY *and* HILDA, *having a row. She holds a battered enamel pisspot.*

STANLEY. I've invited the women to the house-warming.

HILDA. The house isn't ready yet.

STANLEY. It's got a roof, floors! All you want to do is hide away . . . Either that or you're off back to Hampstead –

HILDA. Stanley, they like to see the girls!

STANLEY. You don't paint . . . You're out in that garden, or sewing . . . what are you doing! How can you say you haven't got time for the most important thing about you? The reason I want you! I'm beginning to think the you I believed was you doesn't exist, either that or you pay it so little homage you sin against the Holy Ghost. I'm telling you, Hilda Carline, treat God's gift with reverence or it'll come back like a bullet and smash you in the face. Not to mention what it does to me. (*The baby whimpers. He picks it up, goes on painting, the baby in one arm.*) I mean, never mind me . . . it's all babies now, I'm not saying I mind them but you're not the same – look at you – you're all dropped!

HILDA, *stricken, takes the child from him.*

It's not that I complain, but I must have some pleasure out of life – other people think so . . . I go out of this door people tip their hats, they're proud of me, what's wrong with that, what's more they listen to what I say, they don't keep dropping off to sleep!... you don't even listen to me any more!

HILDA (*tired*). I do, Stan.

STANLEY *works, throws off his shirt . . . works, gets hot again, takes off his trousers and kicks them down. Now he is in a horrible grey vest and sagging pants. He works, gets something wrong, and jumps down from the trestle in fury.*

STANLEY. The trouble is, there's nothing left for Stan! Look at you, you're all . . . you used to wear yellow and put combs in your hair, now it's as though I'm not here, you've made use of me, now I'm in the way, I'm not in the middle of your attention – WHERE I OUGHT TO BE!! How am I supposed to find you the most amazing, wonderful odalisque and heart partner who'll drive me on and up when you look like that? You know, Hilda, I can't always feel like having sex with you if you don't make yourself . . . well – more attractive to me.

HILDA *looks at him in his underwear,*

HILDA. Stanley – Oh, never mind!

STANLEY *moves apart, dresses for his meeting with* PATRICIA. HILDA *lays the baby gently on a rug on the floor, sits and smiles down at the baby.* ELSIE *enters with a basket of clean washing. She stands over* HILDA *and the baby, smiling.*

ELSIE. Look at her little fingers .. ahh!

HILDA (*together*). Ahh!

ELSIE. That wasn't wind.

HILDA. You know she can lift her head now? And say 'Ih'.

ELSIE 'Ih' eh? Well! She'll be on those little feet soon . . .

*(She bends, waggles the baby's foot.)* . . . ah, too pretty to walk on, ahn't they?

HILDA. Much too pretty.

*They lean over the baby as* STANLEY, *passing, tries not to be sick. He escapes.*

## Act One Scene Five

*A party at* STANLEY*'s newly bought house, Lindworth. Food on a sideboard.* ELSIE, *in black dress, white apron and cap, enters with two laden plates, puts them down carefully, stands back to admire the feast. And bumps into* PATRICIA, *dressed as Narcissus and carrying a wand. Behind her is* DOROTHY, *as Oscar Wilde.* ELSIE *shrieks, then recovers apologetically.*

ELSIE. Ooh, I'm sorry, I never recognised you . . . it's Miss . . . ah...?

PATRICIA. The Misses Hepworth and Preece. (*She runs the words together.*)

ELSIE. Sorry?

PATRICIA. The Misses Hepworth and Preece.

ELSIE *still hasn't got it. She backs off with her tray, calls out, announcing* PATRICIA *and* DOROTHY.

ELSIE. The Misses Hepithithiss! (*She goes.*)

PATRICIA *turns, inspects the food on the sideboard.*

PATRICIA. Trifle!

DOROTHY *grins, crosses to look at* STANLEY*'s painting of a river scene with swans.* PATRICIA *joins her.*

PATRICIA. What do you think?

DOROTHY. Rather fine.

PATRICIA (*points*). Me as Mary Magdalene. I can't see the rest of it . . . I mean, where's he been, he's never been anywhere. Sunday painter.

DOROTHY. No, no.

ELSIE *enters with punchbowl, goes.*

PATRICIA (*sniffs*). What's that smell?

DOROTHY. Perhaps they're baking the swan for dinner.

PATRICIA. I hope not.

DOROTHY (*thoughtfully*). No-o. All that neck.

*They turn.* STANLEY *is standing there. He is dressed as* HILDA. *They look at him.*

STANLEY. Well?

*They have no answer to his appearance.*

I like women's clothes.

DOROTHY. Yes. I think Patricia would like a drink, Stanley.

HILDA, *dressed as* STANLEY, *enters, followed by* DUDLEY, HENRY, GWEN *and* AUGUSTUS. *None of the latter are in fancy dress.*

ELSIE. Mr. John, Mr. Tooth, Mr. Lamb and Miss Gwen, I mean Mrs. Raverat.

STANLEY. Didn't you say?

HILDA. Sorry – I forgot.

*She hands* AUGUSTUS *a large drink.* STANLEY *puts up paintings for display.*

AUGUSTUS. Get away from me, you're too fertile . . . (*Collides with* STANLEY.) . . . oh! Who's this little plie de Venus . . . (*Grabs* STANLEY *genially by the neck, nuzzles him.*) How's the breast-feeding . . . ah, the divine Preece! (*He sees the swan painting.*) Ohoho! Hohohohohoho! Bravo, Cookham! That's showing them, eh? (*He digs* STANLEY *in the ribs.*) What have you been up to? (*Gestures at the painting.*)

HILDA *takes* GWEN's *coat.*

HILDA. How are you?

GWEN. Tired. Henry's a morning person.

HILDA. At least he drops off at night. (*She looks over at* STANLEY, *in the distance, discoursing on the picture.*)

GWEN. Still.

HILDA. I know. I glory in him. When he lets me.

STANLEY *moves to a second painting on an easel.* GWEN *smiles at* HILDA, *crosses to join and listen.* HILDA *stands apart.* DUDLEY *sees her, detaches himself politely to join her.*

DUDLEY. It's splendid, isn't it?

HILDA. Oh good, you're pleased.

DUDLEY. Oh indeed . . . why, is there some –

HILDA. No, no. It's just . . . everything is in a bit of a muddle.

DUDLEY, *embarrassed, looks away towards* STANLEY.

DUDLEY. I'll have a word with him.

HILDA. Please.

STANLEY *is standing before a second painting.*

STANLEY. One woman is hanging out washing and a woman over here offers a clothes' basket of cast-offs to the Vicar as some Apostles stop to watch boys playing hopscotch.

PATRICIA. Oh. Which ones are the Apostles?

STANLEY. Here! . . . the ones in holy raiment! – well, some of them are wearing clothes from the basket, taking no thought as to wherewithal they shall be clothed.

PATRICIA *shrugs helplessly at this, irritating* STANLEY.

There's nothing pointless in the notion of disciples watching boys playing hopscotch. Saints and similar species of individuals have a way of being able to contemplate quite simple things in a way as to . . . to make you feel you could contemplate the same thing to the end of time without being bored for one second. Look at that foot! I'm especially good at feet, and the limbs are really limby, don't you think?

AUGUSTUS. Nice stuff, Cook.

STANLEY. Sometimes I like the pigment to sort of stain the canvas rather than sit on it. And diagonals! Usually I hate 'em!

GWEN. It's heavenly, Stanley.

PATRICIA (*drawls, as he looks to her*). We-ell . . . I think . . .

*She keeps him waiting.* DUDLEY *grimaces nervously.*

DUDLEY. Marvellous work. Marvellous.

*But* STANLEY *only has eyes for* PATRICIA.

PATRICIA. . . . I think it's a work of genius.

STANLEY *preens.*

STANLEY. But how does it make you feel? What do you feel – here? (*He claps his heart.*)

PATRICIA (*drawls*). Oh, ecstasy.

*He stands before her, grinning, hands in pockets, rocking back and forth.*

DUDLEY. Splendid stuff, splendid.

GWEN (*kisses him*). No-one works as hard as you, Stanley.

STANLEY. I agree and I'm . . . Now look, I'm not trying to be Michelangelo, well perhaps I am – why not, since I know I'm ready to take on the decoration of a whole church now . . . I could do it in twenty years, if I keep at it . . . every wall, every space . . . A cathedral of me!

*They laugh and clap.* STANLEY *looks across to* HILDA. *She has fallen asleep.* GWEN *takes* STANLEY *away for a drink.* PATRICIA *accosts* DUDLEY.

PATRICIA. Dudley . . . any news?

DUDLEY. I'm sorry?

PATRICIA. You were looking into the possibility of a show for us both.

DUDLEY. I am still making enquiries.

PATRICIA. That was six months ago.

DUDLEY. It's not easy, as you know.

PATRICIA. You manage it for other people.

DUDLEY (*to* DOROTHY). There was some interest in your portraits, Miss Hepworth. I might be able to –

PATRICIA. Oh no. None of that. We show together or not at all.

DUDLEY (*to* DOROTHY) Yes?

DOROTHY (*firmly*). Oh yes.

DUDLEY. Very well, I'll see what I can do.

PATRICIA. Yes, I think you should. Otherwise – Otherwise I shall have to marry that dirty little Stanley Spencer.

DUDLEY *and* DOROTHY *are dumbfounded.*

*Later, the party is drunker and sleepier.*

GWEN (*lying in* HENRY'*s lap*). Ooh no. I'd hate to meet Gauguin on a dark moonless night.

DOROTHY. Ye-es. Not too sure about Bonnard. (*Draws on her cigar.*)

ELSIE *brings in the baby, gives her to* HILDA.

HENRY. 'Je désire . . . mes amis . . . to peek through thee key'ole . . . see women washing themselves like leetul cats.'

DOROTHY. Degas also regretted that he'd thought of women as mere animals.

HENRY. Come on, all artists – well, men . . . (*As* PATRICIA *and* DOROTHY *gaze at him levelly.*) They treat them in different ways.

DOROTHY. Degas treats women as whores, Manet treats whores as women.

DUDLEY. What about old Ingres?

AUGUSTUS. Hah – dilapidated tombstones! (*Laughter.*)

STANLEY. I like French pictures well enough. What I don't understand is why people who rave about them are such Philistines about mine.

*ELSIE enters with coffee. HILDA gives the baby to STANLEY.*

HILDA. Your women are honest, Stanley.

STANLEY. I know that.

HILDA. Coffee . . . Patricia? Stanley?

*She bends cordially. He shakes his head.*

*HILDA and STANLEY are alone. He paces, agitated.*

STANLEY. I don't know what to do, what shall I do?

HILDA. What did she say?

*They pause as ELSIE enters to clear the table. She goes with a tray load.*

STANLEY. She told me to go round.

HILDA. When?

STANLEY. Now.

*Across the stage PATRICIA disrobes and waits, putting lotion on her arms and body.*

HILDA. What did you tell her?

STANLEY. I said I couldn't. I said we had to clear up.

HILDA. Do you want to go?

STANLEY. I don't know. Do you want me to?

*ELSIE enters, relieves STANLEY of the baby, picks up the trifle as well, and goes.*

HILDA. Stanley, I want whatever makes you happy. If you want to go to Patricia you must go. Don't ask my permission.

*He rushes out. We see his face at PATRICIA's window. She turns, but he has disappeared. HILDA starts to clear up but her legs give way. She sits, her face brightens as the door bangs.* PATRICIA *lights up thoughtfully.* STANLEY *stands, scowls at* HILDA, *then rushes out again.* HILDA *is now furious.* STANLEY *walks up and down outside* PATRICIA's *room. She looks across at* DOROTHY *in the shadows, shrugs.* STANLEY *looks in,* PATRICIA *rises. But* STANLEY *has gone.* HILDA *turns as* STANLEY *pads in silently.*

HILDA. What happened? (*Pause.*) Did you sleep with her?

STANLEY. No.

*He sits. She goes, returns with cocoa.*

HILDA. Cocoa?

STANLEY. 'kyou.

HILDA. Biscuit?

*He shakes his head.* HILDA *eats her way through the packet of biscuits.*

HILDA. Was she annoyed?

STANLEY. What?

HILDA. Because you didn't stay?

STANLEY. I don't know. I didn't ask.

*He takes a biscuit absently.*

HILDA. I should think she might be. We might have offended her. She may feel a fool, Stanley. Perhaps you ought to –

STANLEY. What?

HILDA. I don't know.

STANLEY. I saw her through the window. She was on the sofa, she had a glass of brandy in her hand, she has these long fingers . . .

HILDA. I know.

STANLEY. . . . . I must do them . . . and just the one light on, so her shoulders stood out like peeled Comice pears. It broke my heart just to look at her.

HILDA. Oh, Stan.

*Pause.*

STANLEY. She's after me, all right.

HILDA. Perhaps she's sex-starved. That's probably it.

STANLEY. And I'm after her.

*They look at each other, alarmed.*

**Act One Scene Six**

DOROTHY *and* PATRICIA.

DOROTHY. Darling . . . why? It's ridiculous – ludicrous!

PATRICIA. I refuse to be poor –

DOROTHY. That doesn't mean –

PATRICIA. I hate it. I like Things! I must have silk stockings
. . . lingerie, good gloves and shoes. I need hats, I've hardly
one good handbag and nothing at all to wear in the evening
– how am I supposed to go about? You all expect me to –

DOROTHY. What?

PATRICIA. I don't know – to – to Be! Other women have what
they need, it's so unfair.

DOROTHY. Dearest, life's unfair, you –

PATRICIA. I had to go into Woolworths for a Pond's lipstick!
If anyone had seen me, well they wouldn't, they're all in
Bond Street choosing lovely new ensembles for the spring.

*She sniffs.* DOROTHY *puts an arm about her.*

Having to darn blouses, stand over a filthy ironing board –

DOROTHY. You don't do the ironing, I do.

PATRICIA. Well, I won't have it! It's sickening. Don't you
find it sickening?

DOROTHY. Honestly, no.

PATRICIA. No, well, it doesn't really matter to you.

DOROTHY. Whoops!

PATRICIA. Sorry, didn't mean to be rude.

DOROTHY. My dear, I adore you when you're vile, you know that.

PATRICIA. More fool you. (*But she slumps down in front of the sofa on the floor, hugging her teddy bear.*) Perhaps if I take Mr. Bill I can go through with it. (*Pause.*)

DOROTHY. Peggy, you can't! Isn't it better to work . . . to concentrate on your work?

PATRICIA. And what, pray, is the point of that if I can't sell the work because nobody knows me. How are people going to know me if I can't go about because I haven't a decent frock to my back?

DOROTHY. You really think it works like that?

PATRICIA. Oh don't be a fool, of course it does.

DOROTHY. In that case . . . I mean . . . how would someone like Stanley, for example –

PATRICIA. Because he's clever! That silly haircut and talking all the time – those pullovers! He knows what he's doing –

DOROTHY. No, honestly I think –

PATRICIA. Well he can do something for me!

DOROTHY. But dearest girl – why Stanley?

PATRICIA. Because he's there! Really, Hepworth, you can be so puggled sometimes.

DOROTHY (*mutters*). One of us is.

PATRICIA. What? What did you say?

DOROTHY. Nothing.

*She rises from her perch on the back of the sofa.*

Coffee? Horlicks?

PATRICIA. He knows so many people! I'm thinking of you as well as me!

DOROTHY. No, please don't do that. In fact, please, stop it, now.

PATRICIA. Oh, you fool, there's no need to worry. It won't make any difference.

DOROTHY. Won't it?

PATRICIA. Not in the least, not in the slightest. You'll see. I'll have Horlicks. (*As* DOROTHY *goes.*) Big mug!

DOROTHY (*at the door*). You are a tease. Marry Stanley Spencer! You wouldn't be seen dead – I know you . . . and in any case, he's already very and happily married . . . and a papa. Why do I let you do this to me . . . (*Going.*) Big mug, big mug!

*Goes.* PATRICIA*'s face is not humorous.*

**Act One Scene Seven**

PATRICIA *and* STANLEY *in a Moddom shop.*

*They wait, and the* MODDOM *appears with a large box of lingerie. She dips in, holding up lingerie for inspection.*

MODDOM, Apricot? Chartrooz? Eau ne nil?

   PATRICIA *scoops the whole lot up in her arms greedily and retires to change.* STANLEY *clears his throat, half rises. The* MODDOM *smiles condescendingly, picks out a piece of black frilly lingerie.*

MODDOM, Of course, sir.

   STANLEY *nods as the* MODDOM *takes it to* PATRICIA. *They wait.* PATRICIA *emerges in the black.*

MODDOM Ah, now that is . . . (*But she thinks it common.*) . . . Don't you agree, sir?

   STANLEY *nods.* PATRICIA *hands the rest of the lingerie to the* MODDOM.

PATRICIA. I'll have these as well.

MODDOM. All of them? They are pure silk.

PATRICIA. I never wear anything else.

MODDOM (*bowing the neck*). Of course. (*Begins to pack the lingerie.*)

STANLEY. Could you . . . could you . . . (*The women turn on him.*) . . . Could she wear black stockings? (*The women exchange looks.*)

*The moddom, already prepared, proffers the stockings. PATRICIA puts them on. The MODDOM makes out the bill, presents it to STANLEY. He pays with large bank notes from his purse.*

PATRICIA (*preening before him*). Well?

*STANLEY fishes in his coat, produces a long velvet box. Both women leap forward. STANLEY tries to put the necklace around PATRICIA's neck, but he fumbles and they brush him aside. The MODDOM fixes the clasp and holds up a large hand glass for PATRICIA to see herself. STANLEY gazes, mesmerised, as both women feast on the necklace, absorbed and unaware of him. PATRICIA fingers the necklace gently, with a small, rare smile into the glass.*

**Act One Scene Eight**

STANLEY, *on his feet in the studio, is drawing on a large canvas.* HILDA *is posing for him.*

STANLEY. Do you know, I enjoyed doing the nettles!

HILDA. Good.

STANLEY. Perhaps there IS something in landscapes, half a hemisphere of nettles and I discover a planet, usually it's so lonely.

HILDA. Still-life? (*She laughs.*)

STANLEY. This is better. Landscapes . . . ugh! Occasionally you lock into something spiritual, otherwise hopeless. (*He draws rapidly.*) What keeps you going is knowing there's that miraculous spiritual meaning that in a flash can change all the boredom of drawing into a tremendous experience.

HILDA. God steps in and fires you up.

STANLEY. Yes! that's it! Oh, I love talking to you – it's as wonderful as if Saint Peter started speaking in Masaccio's picture of Saint Pete casting his shadow.

*He draws, stands back.*

She let me kiss her you-know-what.

HILDA *does not reply. He looks across at her, draws.*

We're going up to London today.

HILDA. I see.

STANLEY. Don't begrudge, Hilda, I want to buy her some jewels. She's down on her luck.

HILDA. You're making a fool of yourself.

STANLEY. No, I'm not.

HILDA. Well, be careful then. They . . . Patricia may not be what she seems.

STANLEY. She's a lady.

HILDA. I know that. It's . . . she and Dorothy have lived in Paris. They're . . . they're sophisticated.

STANLEY. That is what I find particularly thrilling. The way she talks . . . tantalises . . . I have a passion for female elegance . . . black stockings, high-heels – she wears four inch heels – you never see her going about like an old dish rag, like a shucked bean, like a couple of bamboo sticks tied together . . . she seems to like her body, she preens it at you . . . could you squat down, I want to get the inside of your . . .

HILDA *squats.*

. . . damn, now I'm getting an erection.

HILDA *rises, unbuttoning her blouse.*

HILDA. Do you want – ?

STANLEY. No thanks, I must finish this. The thing is . . .
the thing is I believe it's perfectly possible for me to have a
strong spiritual closeness to more than one woman. I believe
that's absolutely possible and I think . . . it may be necessary
for me to . . . I realise you need to get away from me a lot,
you like to go home with the girls, I know you find me a
strain.

HILDA. Do you want me to go away, is that what you're
saying?

STANLEY. I know my true direction, and I know to a fraction
of an inch when I am deflected.

HILDA. Then you must do what you want. But you must
choose it. You can't ask my permission.

STANLEY. Why not, if that's what I need?

*Silence.*

Aren't you ever attracted to somebody else?

HILDA. No! You are my husband, my one and only, and I am
your wife . . . no-one else can be your real wife, you have no
right to push me out of the way.

STANLEY. Out of the way? – you're never here! The evidence
is, I have a deterrent effect on you. It is very humiliating to
me when all my golden words and interesting remarks only
make you thinner and thinner. I should have thought every
word would add an inch of fat and a tube of rose madder to
your cheeks.

*Moves, looking for charcoals.*

I love being in a room and emanating delicious lovely
'Stanley' qualities, throwing out nice bits of me for people
to pick up . . . I throw something to you and your face is
turned away, when you're not asleep, that is. Perhaps you
don't want to compete – well – I'm sorry – that is mean. I
wouldn't be keen on you at all, physically, if it wasn't for
my spiritual feeling for you. If that begins to whittle down,
well . . .

HILDA. Stanley. Go to London.

STANLEY. You once said that it was a waste that no-one but you could share the wonderful feelings I gave to you –

HILDA. It's all right. If you want to go to London, go.

*He turns away from her, draws obsessively. HILDA gets up, crosses and puts on her hat and coat, picks up her gloves and handbag and crosses to the opposite edge of the stage, where she sits on an upright chair. STANLEY hums away to himself.*

## Act One Scene Nine

STANLEY *and* PATRICIA *in a field of marguerites on a hillside.* STANLEY *is sketching.*

PATRICIA. What are you doing?

STANLEY. Trying to put some order into chaos.

*He rubs out, blows the debris from the paper.*

PATRICIA. Oh, that.

*She suns her face.*

STANLEY. I'm trying . . . to . . . find a difficult problem.

PATRICIA. Why?

STANLEY. Because a problem with an easy answer is not very interesting.

*She rolls over, inspects his drawing.*

PATRICIA. Bushes? I thought you were doing me!

STANLEY. That is my hope and intention. (*Grins.*)

PATRICIA. Fool.

*She lies back, eyes closed. He regards her.*

STANLEY. I wanted to bring you here. Among the marguerites. They're the first things I remember. I remember touching them. The petals. The foxy smell . . . ooooh! . . .

PATRICIA. Monte Carlo would be better.

STANLEY. Miss an English spring? Not me. Wonderful. The first hints, shallots poking through, broad beans showing knobby fists, snowdrops, pussy willow, crocus, then the daffs, the first bluebell, blackbirds starting up five o'clock in the bloody morning . . . and then . . . oh then . . . chickweed, scarlet pimpernel, dandelion, flags, campion, clover, ragged robin, cow parsley . . . I did a painting of some cow parsley with ladies' maids and sorrel, do you want it?

PATRICIA. What size?

STANLEY. Six by eight inches.

PATRICIA. No thanks.

STANLEY. There's a bigger one. Chestnut blossom and leaves.

PATRICIA. That's a small subject, Stanley. You said you'd do more landscapes – you promised!

STANLEY. I'll do the landscapes of your legs – high up.

PATRICIA. It's too early in the day to be dirty.

STANLEY. You liked being in the big picture, didn't you? Eh? Enshrined for posterity?

PATRICIA. Mmmm. I thought the bricks were well done.

STANLEY. You wouldn't have noticed the bloody bricks if you'd liked the picture.

PATRICIA. I'm sorry. It's the weather.

*She rolls over.*

STANLEY. You must love the spring – look at it! I can mix a hundred greens and still find more!

PATRICIA (*jumps up, dusts herself down*). Well, there you are! (*Crosses to him, kisses him lightly.*) I know you don't like painting landscapes, but they sell. Let me take over your affairs, Stanley, then you can concentrate on what you do best, it makes sense. Neither you nor Hilda is good at money. I am. For a start, with Hilda away all the time now, you don't need that big house, you might as well sell it. Better still, put it in my name.

STANLEY *looks up.*

After all, it'll belong to both of us in the end. After the divorce.

STANLEY *puts down his sketching block.*

My dear, you can't possibly spend the rest of your life paying out hard-earned money to keep Hilda – who gives you nothing – and the two girls. Hilda has a very well situated family of her own. Let them look after her. You – are an artist. Your loyalty must – must be to the work. And to me of course. Do you like my red nails?

STANLEY *looks at her spread out hands, then gazes at her face and makes a lunge for her. She flinches and turns away, evading him so that he is only able to kiss the back of her neck. He covers the nape of her neck with kisses. She submits, her face murderous. HILDA, in her hat and coat, with her handbag, sits at the side of the stage.*

HILDA. Can't you come to Hampstead? (*She rises, clumsy in distress.*) It's as though you've dropped a chopper on us without even a thought.

*Across the stage PATRICIA disrobes slowly for STANLEY. She lies on the divan and he starts to draw her.*

STANLEY. I'd like to be an ant crawling all over you.

*He shudders with excitement as PATRICIA laughs.*

HILDA. Stan, please. I can't say I want to go, even for you.

STANLEY *approaches PATRICIA, sits on the divan, kisses her shoulder. She removes his hand. He goes back obediently and starts to draw again, humming happily.*

HILDA. You're my husband. We promised! We took a vow before God to be together forever. Didn't you mean it?

STANLEY, *unable to resist, crosses to PATRICIA, kisses her face feverishly. She tries to turn away.*

STANLEY. Hilda, my feelings have all come alive – it makes me dangerous. (*Across to HILDA.*) You don't want me . . . you don't want Me – Stanley. I could manage twenty wives – why not? (*Groping PATRICIA.*)

HILDA. Please. At least don't say I don't love you. You won't
let me love you, you don't want me to want you so you send
me away. I do as you want because I love you and then you
say I've deserted you.

STANLEY (*raises his head as if from a dream*). Hilda?

PATRICIA *pulls him down into the embrace.*

HILDA. I miss you.

STANLEY *and* PATRICIA *kiss deeply.* HILDA *wipes her
eyes with a large man's handkerchief, blows her nose.*

HILDA. I'm so lonely. I know you don't mean to hurt, you're
just being thoughtless, but oh . . . that's a terrible quality.

PATRICIA, *behind* STANLEY*'s head, looks at her wrist
watch. She tips* STANLEY *off the divan, gestures. He
crosses, picks up his painting things, has too much to carry,
looks round, sees the pram, loads it up, puts on a coat and
muffler, wheels the pram away, sets up his easel.*

STANLEY. You've got the children.

HILDA. A hundred children couldn't replace one Stanley.
Why, my dear . . . why? If I could just see your side.

STANLEY. I've earned her. I deserve her . . . my one social
achievement. I work hard – I'm famous! I get hundreds of
notices. Only yesterday she said she liked the way I was
putting them in my cuttings book, she says things like that,
she's full of compliments, she studies me! To see you trying
to look enthusiastic is so horrible, so bloody insulting, ducky,
that I have to stop whatever I'm doing to let a terrible choking
fit of rage die down – I can't even bear to look at you.

HILDA (*low*). Stan, please . . .

STANLEY (*squirting colours and mixing*). You're not moved
by me. You've no appetite for life – where's your joy? (*He
paints ferociously.*)

HILDA. You are my joy.

STANLEY *returns to* PATRICIA. *He paints himself and*
PATRICIA *in the nude, using a mirror.*

STANLEY. D'you think you could manage on two pounds a
week . . . I haven't been well, I've been losing commissions
. . . no, it's not that, I tell a lie, I want the money to spend
on Patricia. I hate paying out for moral obligation, it's like
Income Tax!

HILDA. Oh no . . .

STANLEY. You're stopping me from doing what I want!

*HILDA is faint. GWEN and HENRY come forward and
support her. GWEN gives her smelling salts, she rallies and
they withdraw.*

HILDA. I'm sorry, Stanley. It's just that I've had a breakdown
in my health. There's something wrong with my eyes, I
can't see. I feel that I don't belong in this world, that I have
no proper place and that I must keep very still and small or
something awful will happen to me and the children. I know
I have a lot to be grateful for but how can we live on so
little? I seem to be in a moon world, full of cold stars, not on
this warm, loving earth at all.

*STANLEY fastens a necklace round PATRICIA's throat.*

STANLEY. Please discontinue writing, your letters will be
returned unopened. In future address all correspondence to
my solicitor. I wish no further connection with you.

*He opens a ring box. PATRICIA takes out the engagement
ring, puts it on her finger, displays it to DOROTHY, who
shrugs and turns away. HILDA, bereft, sits small in her
chair. PATRICIA changes for the wedding. DOROTHY
tries on a hat. PATRICIA shakes her head. STANLEY puts
on a clean shirt, suit and tie.*

HILDA (*very timid*). Am I not worth keeping as a friend? I
went without any fuss. Surely I'm worth something for that?
(*Puzzled.*) How can you be happy when you know I'm in
such plight? What you are doing is murder.

*STANLEY, PATRICIA, DOROTHY and DUDLEY on the
Registry Office steps after their marriage, posing for
pictures. STANLEY is wearing his favourite hat and looks
like Worzel Gummidge. HILDA collapses. GWEN and*

HENRY *carry her out awkwardly, showing her petticoat.*
GWEN *returns for* HILDA*'s handbag. She stands for a
moment, nursing it sadly, then goes.* STANLEY *staggers,
attempting to carry* PATRICIA *over the threshold.*
DOROTHY *follows.* STANLEY, *surprised at* DOROTHY*'s
presence, looks awkward.* DOROTHY, *at* PATRICIA*'s
nod, goes.* STANLEY *can't wait. He pulls off* PATRICIA*'s
clothes, muttering. There is an undignified scrambling on
the divan as* STANLEY *tries to mount* PATRICIA. *She
yelps, jerks away and pushes him off her. She looks at*
DOROTHY, *out of* STANLEY*'s vision, then whispers to*
STANLEY, *taking both his hands and talking urgently. He
seems bewildered. But she goes on whispering, stroking his
hair.*

PATRICIA. Look Stanley, this isn't right, it isn't what you
need – not a great artist like you – for you everything must
be perfect. It's not just me you want – what you need is an
unlimited supply of sex . . . and you can have it!

STANLEY. What you're saying is – ?

PATRICIA. Yes, Stanley! Why not? You are an artist. Why
not? You must have whatever you need . . . if what you need
for happiness is women, women, women . . . Stanley,
(*Whispers in his ear.*) . . . I'll get them for you . . . you shall
have women, as many women as you want . . .

PATRICIA (*looks across at* DOROTHY). Listen, Stanley . . .
I'll make an arrangement with you . . . now, to be fair, we
shouldn't jump the gun, don't you agree? . . . (*She thrusts
him off as he tries to mount her again.*)

STANLEY. Look . . . we're married . . .

PATRICIA. Of course we are . . . (*She waves the marriage
licence at him.*) . . . but let's sort it all out first . . . we don't
want to be unfair to Hilda, you don't want to upset her, do
you . . .

STANLEY. I don't know, I don't think so . . .

PATRICIA. Splendid. So – Dorothy and I will make our way to
St. Ives and you can hang on here –

STANLEY. Why?

PATRICIA. To see her, silly!

STANLEY. Who?

PATRICIA. Hilda. (*As he makes to protest.*) Make an appointment! – ask her down to dinner, she'll come if you invite her, she loves you.

STANLEY (*shakes his head*). She won't come.

PATRICIA. Say you're ill – make some excuse! Meanwhile, Dorothy and I'll open up the house in St. Ives, and you and Hilda can join us for some lovely sea air at your leisure.

*She smiles winningly at* STANLEY, *causing him to jump on her.*

PATRICIA (*calls*). Dorothy, could we have tea and biscuits?

DOROTHY *appears in travelling coat, hat with goggles on forehead and motoring gloves, struggling on with leather suitcases and painting gear.*

DOROTHY. Sorry?

PATRICIA. On second thoughts perhaps we'd better push off, it is a long drive. Let us know when you're coming and we'll meet the Cornish express.

*She kisses* STANLEY *on the cheek and goes with a wave, taking her coat from* DOROTHY, *who smiles apologetically at* STANLEY *and heaves the luggage off. Alone,* STANLEY, *bewildered, picks up his painting things and, looking round, sees the pushchair. He stacks the paints, easel and canvas in the pushchair and wheels it away.*

**Act Two Scene One**

STANLEY'*s studio at Lindworth. A pause.*

HILDA (*off*). Cooee! (*Closer.*) Cooee! (*She enters in her hat and coat. She looks round.*) Hullo . . . (*There is a sound. She turns round and sees STANLEY, which makes her jump.*) Oh, you frightened me.

STANLEY. Hilda?

HILDA. What are you doing here? I'm sorry, I'll go. I didn't know you'd be here, I thought you were going away. I had the letter from Elsie saying she'd packed my things.

STANLEY. Hilda . . .

HILDA. What is it? What's the matter? Why aren't you on your . . . holiday? Is Patricia here?

*He shakes his head.*

HILDA. Where is she?

STANLEY. St. Ives.

HILDA. Oh, I see. No, I don't see. Why is she in St. Ives and you – ?

STANLEY. It's all right, she's with Dorothy.

*He takes HILDA's hands, draws her down, they sit.*

HILDA. What is it? What's the matter, Stanley?

STANLEY. I've been waiting for you. Look.

*He jumps up, sets a painting on the easel. He shows her one painting after the other. He puts up the last one. Silence. HILDA nods.*

HILDA. You've been taking risks.

STANLEY. Dudley says people will think them dirty. He says they won't sell.

HILDA *does not reply. She looks at the pictures propped up, turning her head.*

What do you think?

*Hilda looks at the nudes of* STANLEY *and* PATRICIA.

HILDA. I think they're very tender.

STANLEY. I knew you'd understand. I've missed you so much.

HILDA. You know I've missed you.

STANLEY. I didn't mean it, any of it. Patricia said I had to say all those things, for the divorce.

HILDA. Stanley, that's no excuse.

STANLEY. I know. Wait! (*He rushes out and runs back in with dishes of food decorated with flowers, making several journeys. He lays the dishes around her at her feet.*) All your favourites. Cherries, Spanish cheese, shepherd's pie, Marmite toast.

HILDA. I'm not very –

*But he kneels before her, a dish in each hand. She takes something in each hand, tries to eat. She has trouble swallowing.*

Could I – could I have a drink of water?

STANLEY. Ooh, I forgot! Look! (*He brandishes a jug of barley water and two glasses.*)

*Later.* HILDA, *now relaxed, sits with* STANLEY. *They have drunk the barley water.*

HILDA. Your dear, dear face. Oh Stanley, I've been so hungry! (*They kiss. He breathes deep, sniffs her.*)

STANLEY. It's all right, you smell just the same . . . beech nuts and broom flower . . . ohhh . . . (*He kisses her again, begins to fondle her.*)

HILDA. Stanley, can we?

*He groans, buries his face in her bosom.* HILDA *sighs deeply, and holds him to her passionately.*

## Act Two Scene Two

*The sound of gulls.* DOROTHY *and* PATRICIA *are on the beach at St. Ives. They wear sunhats and are sitting on small folding chairs, working at easels, painting seascapes.* PATRICIA *stops work.*

PATRICIA. This is absolute bliss.

*She looks across at* DOROTHY, *who is absorbed in her work.*

Why work so hard? Stop . . . breathe . . . enjoy life.

DOROTHY (*still working*). Consider the lilies?

PATRICIA (*groans*). Don't – you sound like Stanley Spencer.

DOROTHY. Your husband.

PATRICIA. At least we've got a decent property now.

DOROTHY. We're staying on at Moor Thatch, aren't we?
    That's what you said! (*Alarmed, she puts down her brush.*)

PATRICIA. Of course.

DOROTHY. They why do we need Stanley's house?

PATRICIA. Income, silly! Somebody has to think of the future.

DOROTHY (*puzzled*). Income . . . ?

PATRICIA. That house will let at a very decent rent.

DOROTHY. Are you saying that the only reason you married –
    I thought it was . . . I know you love a name . . . I don't
    know what to think! I can't sleep!

PATRICIA. Don't I know! You've been sweating like a back
    rasher . . . muttering in the night. It's all very well, what
    about me, I need sleep too, you know. I'm liable to get ratty.

DOROTHY. Sorry. (*She comes over to look at* PATRICIA*'s work.*) It's good. Coming on.

PATRICIA. It's finished!

DOROTHY. Oh.

PATRICIA. I said we'd have drinks with Barbara.

DOROTHY (*shakes her head*). Too much to do.

PATRICIA. Oh come on, this is supposed to be a holiday!

DOROTHY. What it is supposed to be, is your honeymoon.

DOROTHY *walks apart and gazes out to sea, her back to* PATRICIA.

DOROTHY. Couldn't we go away? France perhaps . . .

PATRICIA. That's an idea! I thought about our staying on here but they're such an obsessive lot. Me for the Riviera.

DOROTHY. Or there's Italy . . . Verona, Siena . . .

PATRICIA. What about Capri? We could live for nothing. Stanley's rents would be more than enough –

DOROTHY. No.

PATRICIA. Why not?

DOROTHY. It's out of the question. (*She begins to pack her things. Straightens up.*) I may go alone. Abroad. (*Silence.*)

PATRICIA. I'd rather you didn't.

DOROTHY. Then please don't ask me to live off Stanley Spencer.

PATRICIA. Suit yourself . . . it's my money, I'll spend it as I please. I'm the one who married him, what have you done towards it?

DOROTHY. How can you think of taking that man's house! I have to stand by and watch you – cavort – in order to get him to sign over his own home to you –

PATRICIA. I do not cavort.

DOROTHY. Then why has he done it? Don't tell me he's had nothing from you –

PATRICIA. Are you accusing me of selling myself? I am not a whore.

DOROTHY. Then you've defrauded him.

PATRICIA. I – am – doing – this – for – you! That little madman is perfectly capable of making up his own mind. If he chooses to help two artists, two painters of repute, then that is his privilege.

DOROTHY. You'd do the same yourself.

PATRICIA. What?

DOROTHY. If you were in his position.

PATRICIA. If I were in his position the first thing I would do is get a decent address. If I am – if I were – which I'm not – about to take on the role of hostess for him – introduce him to –

DOROTHY. The right circles?

PATRICIA. Don't worry. I'm not going to.

DOROTHY. I don't know what to believe. Except that you'll use him to beat me over the head with. (*She sits, feeling weak.* PATRICIA *sits beside her.*)

PATRICIA. Dodo, he hasn't even touched me. I promise. Well not down there.

DOROTHY. I can't bear to think of his hands on you.

PATRICIA (*shudders*). Nor me.

DOROTHY. Then what in the name of God, Peggy – ?

PATRICIA. Don't worry, everything is arranged. I've said they can live in the studio.

DOROTHY. Arranged? By whom?

PATRICIA. I'm prepared to sit for him, and that's it.

DOROTHY. And he's agreed – not to touch you?

PATRICIA. Leave it to me – you're shivering!... in the sun! Dodo! Here, have my jacket and stop worrying. Just get on with the work, leave all the rest to me. Please!

*She strides off forcefully, leaving* DOROTHY *to bring all the things.*

**Act Two Scene Three**

HILDA *and* STANLEY *come out into the garden with a tray of coffee and a plate of buns. They sit in basket chairs, and eat and drink in cheerful silence and with hearty appetites.*

HILDA. Mmmmm!

STANLEY. Manage another?

HILDA (*mouth full*). Mmm.

> *She takes another large bun. Bird song.* HILDA *refills their cups. They finish their coffee together, the cups go down together.* HILDA *lies back, closing her eyes and lifting her face to the sun.* STANLEY *leans over the table, looking at her and smiling.* HILDA *sits up suddenly.*

STANLEY. What?

HILDA. You don't think what we've just done's adultery, do you?

STANLEY. We-ell –

HILDA. You don't, do you, Stan?

STANLEY. I don't see how it can be.

HILDA. It can! We're not married!

STANLEY. We are. In the eyes of God we are.

HILDA. No we're not. We're divorced. The Church of England allows divorce and we're divorced. We're not Catholics.

STANLEY. No. Pity. Let's change.

HILDA. Oh, Stan.

> *Silence between them. Birdsong. She leans across the garden table and takes his hand.*

HILDA. Shall I tell you something? I don't care if it is.

STANLEY. What?

HILDA. Adultery.

STANLEY. Good. Good! (*He jumps up, excited.*) Good! (*He plucks a branch from a tree, capers round her.* HILDA *laughs, throws a bun at him. He fetches up before her, triumphant.*) You don't know how pleased that makes me.

HILDA. Never mind you, what about me . . . I'm a fallen woman. Oh dear.

STANLEY. What is it?

HILDA. Patricia. How are we going to tell her? Oh Stan, we can't build happiness on somebody else's misery. It doesn't work, honestly.

STANLEY. No, that's all sorted out, everything's arranged. Patricia's all right.

HILDA. What do you mean? You mean she's left you? You've only just got –

STANLEY. No, no, no, no, no. She's agreed!

HILDA. Agreed to what?

STANLEY. She's even invited us to St. Ives, together!

HILDA. What? I . . . I don't know what to say. When did she – ?

STANLEY. She telephoned yesterday –

HILDA. Why did you? When did you . . . ? And there's no bad feelings?

STANLEY. None at all! She says I'm an artist, I must have what I need, what's necessary. You're necessary! And the girls of course, how are they?

HILDA. They're fine. Stan, does this mean we're a family again? I can come back?

STANLEY. I should think so. Patricia doesn't want to move in here, she wants to stay at the cottage with Dorothy. I shouldn't think she'd mind your being here, no, I'm sure she wouldn't; she likes your cooking.

HILDA. Stanley. I don't think I've got this clear. Could you explain it to me?

STANLEY. There's nothing to explain. It's all arranged!

HILDA. Are you sleeping with her?

STANLEY. Who?

HILDA. Patricia, who did you think I meant!

STANLEY. Not as such.

HILDA. Either you are or you aren't.

STANLEY. She wants to wait. Until you and I are sorted out. To tell the truth we've had some . . . difficulties.

HILDA. What sort of difficulties?

STANLEY. She can't manage it. There's something wrong with her.

HILDA. You mean you haven't been to bed with her? Not at all?

STANLEY. Not as such.

HILDA. Don't keep saying that!

STANLEY. So the arrangement is –

HILDA. Arrangement? Whose arrangement?

STANLEY. Patricia thinks . . . she's being very generous about this. She knows I love you.

HILDA. What arrangement? What arrangement, Stanley?

STANLEY. That I can be married to both of you. She says when you and I are . . . together again, she'll . . . she and I can . . . we can do it too. I can have her as well. This is what I want, it's what I need. She understands that. She's not conventional, she's an upper class woman.

HILDA. So you're saying . . . what you're saying is . . . after all this dreadful misery, you throwing me off, and saying you never wanted to see me again, that you hated me, that I was boring and ugly and made you feel low and unloved and unsupported and that I was an utter disappointment, now you say you didn't mean any of that, you say you love me and want me here, in my own home again . . . at least you think you want me, if Patricia allows it, you want me here . . . back as I was before . . . as your mistress.

*Silence.*

Is that what you mean, Stanley?

STANLEY. Put like that, yes.

HILDA *tips over the table, throwing the breakfast things on the ground.*

HILDA. I don't know which one of you I want to kill first.

*He comes towards her.*

No, no more, Stanley

*She turns away, rage evaporating into pain, as* ELSIE *runs on.*

HILDA (*to* ELSIE). I'll write to you about my things. Thank you for packing them up. I'll arrange for a carrier.

*She goes.* STANLEY *stands, bewildered. Slowly he starts to pick up the things on the ground. Birdsong.*

## Act Two Scene Four

AUGUSTUS JOHN's *studio.* AUGUSTUS, *in a filthy old smock, is at the easel, painting, a clay pipe clamped between his teeth. A sound makes him look up.* STANLEY *is there.*

AUGUSTUS. What are you doing here?

STANLEY *does not reply,* AUGUSTUS *carries on working.*

What do you want?

STANLEY. Nothing.

(*After a pause.*) I was just thinking.

AUGUSTUS. What?

STANLEY. You know about women.

I've tried to talk to her.

AUGUSTUS. Which one? Peggy or Hilda?

STANLEY Augustus, I don't know if being divorced is colouring my outlook . . . perhaps I'm becoming a libertine . . .

*He pauses, intrigued by the idea.* AUGUSTUS *chuckles.*

Well, whatever I am, I'm sure it's good. What I want to
know is, why must a man have only one woman? Apart
from the expense. I'm divorced from Hilda now, but I'm as
much hers as ever. I see Patricia every day, I hope I always
shall, but the one doesn't cut across the other ... I mean,
why all this possessive business?

AUGUSTUS. Oh, I don't stand for that.

STANLEY. I suppose I must be polygamous if I want more
than one wife but I don't see why that should be derogatory.
I think it's a sign of intelligence. I can reach the most
intense state of being and awareness, and in each case it is
utterly sincere. I feel total fusion and ecstasy with Hilda ...
and with Patricia.

AUGUSTUS. Yes ... bravo, Cookham.

STANLEY. Intimacy is important, don't you agree?

AUGUSTUS. Absolutely.

STANLEY. Why should I be deprived of her? My closest partner? Simply because a piece of paper says we're divorced?

AUGUSTUS. Bugger the law.

STANLEY. Exactly. My art is being interfered with! I need a
dozen homes – that's what I'd like, with me as father in
each. That's why men get irritable, they want a change of
wife, maybe for just a short time. (*He groans.*) When I think
of all the women I might have known!

AUGUSTUS. Spunky little turps-rag like you should be
ranging the hills like a white-assed collie!

STANLEY. D'you think so?

AUGUSTUS. You want to know the secret, my boy? To the
female sex?

STANLEY (*miserable*). I wish you'd tell me.

AUGUSTUS. Surprises. They like surprises. Unpredictability,
that's my advice to you.

STANLEY *digests this.* AUGUSTUS *refills his pipe, picks
up his brush. Then grabs a turps rag, swipes at the picture
irritably.* STANLEY *leans over his shoulder for a look.*

AUGUSTUS. Needs more work.

STANLEY. Yes it does.

AUGUSTUS. That's because she's an ugly bitch. Need to pretty her up.

STANLEY. I don't see why you have to do all this society stuff.

AUGUSTUS. Five hundred guineas for this. And I can knock it off in a week.

STANLEY. No wonder it's no good.

AUGUSTUS. You're asking for a clip round the ear.

STANLEY. Is this what you want to be known by?

AUGUSTUS. Chapel-going little bible thumper –

STANLEY. It's a lie.

AUGUSTUS. Coming in here – piss off, scram!

STANLEY (*banging his chest*). You used to paint from here –

AUGUSTUS. Go on - bugger off! Scram!

STANLEY (*grabbing a bottle of whisky*). Now it's from here!

*There is a tussle as* AUGUSTUS *wrests the bottle from* STANLEY, *takes a good sized drink.*

AUGUSTUS. I can't do it any more.

STANLEY. I don't know what I'd do if I couldn't work. I don't think I could bear it. I miss her.

AUGUSTUS. Old Hilda? Dammit, man . . . what you've got to do is get round her. Tell her she's beautiful . . . the loveliest physog in Christendom – neck like a Delft jug, bum like a Boucher . . . Hilda de Milo . . . the Rokeby Hilda . . . Hilda of Troy!

STANLEY. I couldn't do that. I couldn't lie to Hilda.

*He stands, then goes.* AUGUSTUS *attacks the canvas, then throws down the brush in disgust.*

**Act Two Scene Five**

HILDA's *family home in Hampstead.* HILDA *is sitting, hands clasped. Her mother,* MRS. CARLINE, *eccentrically dressed in an artistic manner, enters.*

MRS. CARLINE. He's here. (HILDA *shows alarm.*) In the lavatory. I'd no intention of upsetting him. I merely remarked that 'what therefore God hath joined together, let not man put asunder'. Chastity, Stanley . . . (*As* STANLEY *enters.*) is the cement of civilisation and progress.

STANLEY. Yes, well I didn't –

MRS. CARLINE. Without it one cannot attain the Science of Life.

STANLEY. I didn't know you were going to be here. I thought it was to be just Hilda.

MRS. CARLINE. I am here as the wakeful shepherd.

STANLEY. Oh yes?

MRS. CARLINE. The protection of those that are bruised is –

STANLEY. Bruised?

MRS. CARLINE. Stanley, someone must protect Hilda's interests.

STANLEY. Yes. Me. (*Silence.*)

MRS. CARLINE. As to that, all unspoken thoughts are known to the Divine Mind. However, you may rest assured, Hilda has not discussed her private affairs with me.

STANLEY. Why not?

MRS. CARLINE. I have no wish to pry into the intimate details of –

STANLEY. Why not? You ought to. Put your oar in – she's your daughter. I don't understand you lot.

*Pause.*

MRS. CARLINE. Very well. Hilda is unhappy.

STANLEY. Well, there's no need for that.

MRS. CARLINE. Splendid! Let every valley of sin, every mountain of selfishness be brought low and the highway to God be prepared for Science. Sherry?

STANLEY (*shakes his head irritably*). No, and I do wish you wouldn't keep bringing God into it. I don't see where He belongs in all this . . . if you don't mind my saying so. I know He's in everything and all that sort of business, but there are times when you just want to be left to get on with it . . . without God there in the way blinding you with His light. It can get on your nerves. I'm not saying you're wrong, Ma C, or that I blame you for it, but there's no doubt about it, you do put God first sometimes . . . most of the time, in fact. Your God, that is.

MRS. CARLINE. MY God, Stanley? Pray, what do you mean – 'MY God'?

STANLEY. Perhaps that's it. Perhaps that's where the confusion comes in. We all see Him differently. Perhaps that's why He's made us all separate . . . He's done it on purpose so's we all get a piece of the ineffable – a fraction of light.

MRS. CARLINE. No doubt. Stanley, why are you here and what is the position with the second Mrs. Spencer?

STANLEY. I love her and I want Hilda to love her.

MRS. CARLINE. Caritas, one presumes – not eros.

STANLEY. Both . . . both . . . both . . . She is delicious – she shines . . . there's a radiance . . . she is mysterious . . . she glides into a room like a dace through a willow pond, her arms are like peeled alder, the air goes arabesque, Bach becomes Borodin. She moves my imagination.

*A silence.* MRS. CARLINE *glances briefly at* HILDA, *who sits, immobile and without expression.*

MRS. CARLINE. I daresay.

*Silence.* STANLEY *and* HILDA *do not look at each other.*

Well it can't go on.

*Silence.* MRS. CARLINE *rises, crosses and stands over* STANLEY.

Stanley, if you are not prepared to wait patiently on divine wisdom to point out your path then . . . well . . . it's a frightful mess, but you had better say goodbye to Hilda, your true wife, here and now. And your children.

HILDA. He doesn't want them.

STANLEY. Oh come on, I've never made a fuss, I'm very good with the girls, better than –

HILDA. You resent them. You resent the time I spend with them . . . look at your face. You . . . who talk and talk and talk of your own family, your parents, your brothers, your beloved sisters –

STANLEY. Yes because they Were me, they Are me –

HILDA. Yet you're jealous of your own girls, your own flesh!

STANLEY. I've never minded. You wanted children – all right –

HILDA. Yes! I wanted children! All the genius in the world can't alter the fact that I'm a woman. I like children. They engage me. They are beautiful . . . unexpected . . . You talk endlessly of you and me . . . me/you . . . What are the children if they are not US? How can that not move you? They are so Exciting! New!

STANLEY (*another thought occurring*). Ah – new! Hilda –

HILDA. They make me unselfish. Stanley, without children we die. In more ways than one.

STANLEY (*urgent*). Hilda –

MRS. CARLINE, *seeing his warmth, smiles.*

MRS. CARLINE. Dear hearts. Perhaps we should dwell silently on conjugal felicity.

*She stands, hands clasped, inviting them to join her in silent prayer. HILDA rises, closes her eyes. STANLEY joins in. Restless, he opens his eyes, waits for it to be over.*

Amen.

HILDA. Amen.

STANLEY. Amen.

*Silence. STANLEY peeks, makes a false rise. MRS CARLINE rises, puts a hand on their heads, goes. They get up.*

STANLEY. Still the same old Ma. (*He walks about rapidly.*) Hilda – do you know something? (*He plonks himself before her triumphantly.*) The whole of my life in art has been a slow realisation of the mystery of sex! It's the key to everything!

HILDA. I miss your face so much.

STANLEY. Yes of course – I'm discovering a hoard of significant meaning . . . I feel like Isaac Newton.

Hilda, I am convinced that the erotic is the essence of religion. I intend to spend the rest of my life reaching the spiritual through the phyisical . . . that personal experience you get when you draw someone's body – isn't that the most wonderful sexual experience? Wait till you see my Beatitudes! I've been working every hour – day and night! I'm getting it all down . . . not just sex . . . living, loving, playing, sharing, marriage, women, loving – did I say loving?

You can't just abandon me.

I've done you as Juno, Goddess of Motherhood and as Athena, Goddess of Wisdom, and I've done . . . (*Catches himself up.*). . . others as other people. Come home.

HILDA. Stanley, please. How can I?

STANLEY. Why not? People can think what they want.

HILDA. No, no . . . don't misunderstand, I'm not in the least conventional, surely you know that, it wouldn't matter to me in the slightest what people said.

STANLEY. Good, because I need you.

*She shakes her head,*

Why not?

HILDA. Because –

STANLEY (*getting ratty*). Because what?

HILDA. Because life on a daily basis – there wouldn't BE life on a daily basis. Sometimes you . . . then . . . the children and I . . . and you not there, but somewhere else. With someone else.

STANLEY. You told me to go if I wanted. To have her.

HILDA. I know. And I wouldn't have minded! If that was truly what you needed. But not total invasion and destruction. All the lovely pace and rhythm of our life jangled like a smashed up milk cart.

STANLEY. It won't be like that. Not if you come back. We'll arrange it to suit you. Fit round you.

HILDA *smothers a spurt of rage.*

HILDA. Please, Stanley. I've had to try and remake my life on the basis of being completely cut off from you – of your having no pleasure or interest in me, and more or less hating me. I've had to build these thoughts into my life, I've been torn from you forcibly, like a branch. Now . . . well, it would need the most enormous graft. You've held all the cards, you know I was always yours. But I've had to face the fact that although you would always be my husband, I was not, you made it clear, any longer your wife. I've had to wean myself from you.

And I'm replaceable. We both know it. You are irreplaceable to me, but there it is. And what about Patricia? Do you really think that if I came back in your life it wouldn't affect Patricia? That she really wants me living down the road from her? As a fill in, because she doesn't want to or can't sleep with you? What's the matter with her? Tell her to see a doctor!

STANLEY. No, please, we can't stop now . . . there's no sense of reality in our being apart. I can't conceive it, I never have. Nobody else could be as we are . . . as we've been. Everyone else is out there . . . even Patricia – I like her for it, it leaves me alone. But not you. How can you leave me, you are me.

HILDA. I know.

STANLEY. What I want – what I need is for you to accept me as I am, who I am, what I am. I want you to accept that I need to be with other women. If only I could make you understand! A new experience means a greater understanding of the old experience. I can please you more now – I know more. I've never not wanted you. Never.

HILDA (*begins to soften*). Oh Stanley . . .

STANLEY. Look – it's all right. Patricia says it's fine, I can have as many women as I want!

HILDA. And is . . . is she to have the same freedom? To go with as many men as she wants?

STANLEY. No, she only wants me.

HILDA. But you wouldn't mind . . . if she did want other men?

STANLEY. It doesn't come into it! Look . . . everything's arranged. She doesn't mind in the least . . . she likes you!

HILDA *gets up and goes.*

## Act Two Scene Six

GWEN's *house. A doorbell rings.* BETTY, *the maid, crosses to open the front door as* GWEN *prepares for guests.*

BETTY. Go away. No, you can't come in. Go on, clear off. Go on, off my steps, get off with you.

GWEN. It's all right, Betty. It's Mr Spencer.

STANLEY *comes in. He is wearing his old favourite hat, an old coat fastened with a large safety pin.*

STANLEY. Sorry. Am I early?

GWEN. Yes you are. Doesn't matter. Stanley, you look awful. How's Patricia?

STANLEY. I don't know. She won't let me in the house.

GWEN. Why not?

STANLEY. Because Hilda won't come back. Could you persuade her, Gwen. She'll listen to you.

GWEN. Stanley, I love you, you know that. I revere your work, you know that. But you mustn't ask this. I can't go to Hilda for you.

STANLEY. What's wrong with all you women! You'll all of you do things on the sly. Oh yes . . . creeping round the back door, but to be out in the open, the way I am, no, no. I am not going to be a liar. I can't do my work and have all this . . . I must have things clear.

GWEN. The way you want it, you mean.

STANLEY. It's the way all men want it if they'd only be honest and speak up. I'd like twenty wives . . . I want to be able to go from one house to another . . . be made welcome . . . I'd like to – when one of them isn't, or when . . . or having children . . . anyway, you feel more alive when . . . it's getting in the way all this, and now Dudley's worried, just when I need the money, he says he can't sell my work!

GWEN. Why not?

STANLEY. He says people think it's dirty.

GWEN (*puzzled*). Dirty?

STANLEY. Do you think I paint dirty pictures?

GWEN. What does he mean?

STANLEY. Erotic. He means erotic. I've been painting Patricia in the nude.

GWEN. Hardly avant-garde.

STANLEY. Ah, but these are too real. Pubic hair, Creases. Buttocks.

GWEN. How disgusting. I mean, that they're not selling. I mean, that they're not selling, Stanley.

STANLEY. Dudley says people are easily shocked – well, in this country.

GWEN. I know. It's the cold weather. They aren't used to being without clothes, so they're more easily surprised.

STANLEY. She sends me out all the time to do landscapes to pay her bills –

GWEN. You mean Patricia?

STANLEY. She won't let me in the cottage. I'm only allowed in the kitchen.

GWEN. She's in the cottage? Not with – ?

STANLEY. With Dorothy.

GWEN. So where are you, are you – ?

STANLEY. At Lindworth. Well, in the studio, not in the house. She's let that.

GWEN *bursts out laughing.*

GWEN. Poor old Stanley. (*She tries to stop but the sight of* STANLEY *sets her off again.*) What . . . oof . . . what does Hilda say?

STANLEY. That she wants to shoot me.

GWEN. Good, I'll get the cartridges.

*The doorbell goes.* DUDLEY *and* HENRY *enter.* BETTY *enters with drinks, pours and takes them round.*

HENRY. Stanley, is that you?

STANLEY. Of course it's me, who d'you think it is?

HENRY. I thought it was Dan, Dan, the dirty old man!

DUDLEY *restrains* STANLEY *as he makes for* HENRY.

GWEN. Are you staying in London?

STANLEY. No. I'll probably miss the last train. I'll sleep on the station.

GWEN. Don't be silly. You'd better stay here. I must dress.

*She goes, followed by* BETTY. *Silence.* STANLEY *glowers.*

HENRY. Well, for God's sake, you don't have to go round like that. We all know . . . you don't have to broadcast –

DUDLEY. Henry . . .

HENRY. What does he think he's playing at?

DUDLEY. Look, Stanley has a lot of worrying problems.

HENRY. You bet he has!

STANLEY. Been talking to Hilda? Oh I know! Simply because I'm trying to be honest.

HENRY. What do you want to do that for? (*He stretches back, lights a cigarette.*)

STANLEY. I come from an honest house. I won't say I'm a Christian, that's too orthodox. But if the synonym God is Love is Christian, well, I'm for that –

HENRY. So it seems. Doesn't mean to say you can run around like a rampant terrier.

STANLEY. Unlike the rest of you, I'm treating . . . trying to treat women well. Openly. With some sort of fairness. I've always been like that. I don't trim, I know you middle classes are all the same, separate bedrooms, ooh, don't come too close, never look you in the eye, you must all be experts on foreheads, it's what you look at when you talk. Well, I'm not like that, and I won't be, and I don't desire to be.

HENRY. You're straightforward. 'Good old Stan . . . always the same. Not jumped up, give you the time of day, modest old Stan.' Forgive me, my dear chap, but bollocks!

DUDLEY. Now Stanley –

*As* STANLEY *makes a lunge at* HENRY.

HENRY. You court simplicity like a dog after a bitch. The bitch is barren, my friend. You think you need to be simple to be clear, here . . . (*Pointing to his temple.*) . . . to guard the shrine, tend the talent. Well, who am I to say?

DUDLEY. Perhaps Stanley's instinct is sound. His life at Cookham has been the source of so much fine work.

STANLEY. But not now. Now I'm painting pornography.

DUDLEY. I saw the picture of you and Patricia.

STANLEY. And?

HENRY. I wish I could afford to buy it.

STANLEY. Thank you.

*He breaks down and cries.* DUDLEY *gives him a handkerchief.*

DUDLEY (*moved*). It's all right, Stanley, it's all right.

STANLEY *cries.*

### Act Two Scene Seven

*At Moor Thatch. A tea-table, laid.* HILDA *sits at the table in hat and coat, clutching her handbag.* DOROTHY *enters with a teapot, pours and sits.*

DOROTHY. It's very good of you.

HILDA. You asked me, Dorothy, and I'm here.

DOROTHY. How are you?

HILDA. You're thinner.

DOROTHY. Yes. I've lost weight.

*She passes* HILDA *a cup of tea. Offers a plate of sand-wiches,* HILDA *shakes her head. She drinks tea, or tries to. Her hands shake.* DOROTHY *takes the cup.*

DOROTHY. My dear Hilda . . .

HILDA *fishes in her handbag for a large white handkerchief, silently wipes her eyes. And rises, aghast, as* PATRICIA *enters quickly.* PATRICIA *pushes her down, sits beside her.*

PATRICIA. Hilda, I do absolutely need a word with you.

DOROTHY. Patricia, please.

HILDA, *stunned, stares up at* PATRICIA.

PATRICIA (*grabbing a piece of cake*). Mmm – cherry cake!

DOROTHY *pours* PATRICIA *a cup of tea.*

HILDA. Is Stanley here?

PATRICIA. No, he's out painting a woman copulating with the war memorial.

HILDA. Did he ask you to invite me here today?

DOROTHY. No.

PATRICIA. No, no, no, no, no. Absolutely not, it was my idea. Hilda – delicious cake Hepworth – (*To* HILDA.) Won't you reconsider coming back to Cookham? It is your home, after all. You shouldn't have gone away so much! I did resist, you know. You may not believe me, but it's true. He's very forceful, it tires one out.

HILDA. I know. But you see, Stanley puts in everything, in everything he does. Because of that he expects –

PATRICIA. He feels he can behave badly!

*She drinks her tea.*

HILDA. No. He simply doesn't think.

PATRICIA. Well, someone must! We're in the same boat, you and I. Made use of for his . . . purposes and for his pathological, hideous paintings . . . I look preposterous. There is a dark side to Stanley you know nothing about . . .

HILDA *tries to rise.* PATRICIA *pulls her down.*

PATRICIA. Please . . . I'm on your side. Really. We both are.

*Holds out her cup.* DOROTHY *rises, takes out the teapot for more hot water.*

We're on the same side. Can't we solve this . . . together?

*Silence.* HILDA *speaks in a low voice.*

HILDA. I will consider coming back to Cookham. If you will agree to leave Stanley.

PATRICIA. Leave?

HILDA. Divorce him.

PATRICIA. Oh, no, I couldn't possibly do that.

HILDA. Why not?

PATRICIA. Apart from anything else I should have to name
you as co-respondent. I couldn't do that to you, Hilda. I have
much too much respect for you. And the children.

DOROTHY, *re-entering with the pot, stops short. And goes
out again.*

HILDA. Then, if you won't divorce him, will you agree to go
away? Give me back my house and leave Stanley alone?

PATRICIA. May I remind you that you are speaking to his
legal wife? There's no question of my conveying Lindworth
back to you . . . totally impossible.

HILDA. Why?

PATRICIA. We need the income from the rent, to live on.

HILDA. But it isn't yours!

PATRICIA. Of course it's mine! I don't mind your renting
back some of the effects, or any small thing of sentimental
value . . . I've already allowed Stanley some pieces for the
studio.

HILDA (*bravely*). I should like my linen, please. And the
china.

PATRICIA. I'm afraid it's all in use. Stanley comes in for
tea . . . he brings friends, often without appointment!

HILDA. May I have my things, please?

PATRICIA. You were using double damask table napkins as
paint rags! Nothing's worth anything, I can read *The Times*
through the sheets and as for the china – did you ever have a
decent dinner service?

*Silence.* DOROTHY *enters, steps back as* PATRICIA *waves
her away.*

Won't you reconsider? It's putting me in such a bad light.
Nobody in the village will speak to me, I'm having a horrible

time. It's different for Stanley, with no background – in any
case, he's home and dry . . . he sells! But even if he didn't,
he has nowhere to fall, d'you see?

Won't you come back . . . he's so miserable. Can't you do it
for him? Come back? If people saw us arm in arm – at least
talk to him.

*Pause.*

HILDA. I don't know Stanley any more. He sent me the most
dreadful letters. Now when I write he never replies.

PATRICIA. He really has no time at all, he's finding it hard to
work and he must, to pay for everything. If you were to
come back, so that he could get down to it –

HILDA. Does he read my letters?

PATRICIA. He's too busy. (*Reassuringly.*) I do!

HILDA. You read my letters to Stanley!

PATRICIA. I'm his wife. I open all his correspondence.

HILDA *looks at her, with dawning awareness.*

HILDA. And his letters to me?

PATRICIA. Naturally I dictated them. I have to protect his
interests, but that's beside the point. Please come back. It
would clear the atmosphere . . . solve everything . . .
Dorothy and I could get on with our lives.

HILDA. You say you are his wife. But you don't live with him.
He says there is nothing . . . that you and he . . . I've always
known that you and Dorothy . . . that you . . . you live a
more sophisticated life . . . you've lived in Paris . . . but if
that's the case and you don't want him . . . don't want your
closeness to Miss Hepworth to be invaded . . . then what is
Stanley to you but a means of paying your debts!

PATRICIA. Oh, for Heaven's sake. We're Artists! We're not
conventional people! Look, if you insist I'll throw in the bed
linen and the china – well, some of it. I can't say fairer than
that – it's against my own interest!

HILDA *rises. Shakily, she picks up the teapot by mistake.*

DOROTHY *appears, gives* PATRICIA *a sharp look, helps* HILDA *out, taking the pot gently from her and giving her her handbag. We hear them murmuring goodbyes.* DOROTHY *enters.*

PATRICIA. She won't have it.


## Act Two Scene Eight

HILDA *and* DUDLEY *in the mental home.* DUDLEY *walking up and down.* HILDA *looks pale and distraught. Her face is white and her hair looks odd.*

HILDA. How is he?

DUDLEY. Not very well.

HILDA. Oh?

DUDLEY. I don't mean ill. How are you?

HILDA. Not very well.

*Silence.*

He wrote me a letter. (*She clutches the letter.*) He wants to come and see me.

*Silence. Then as* DUDLEY *makes to speak.*

He always said he wanted to marry me from the first day he saw me. The thought of marriage never entered my head. He was so jealous of the babies. (*She looks in her lap, twiddling her fingers.*) Is he well?

DUDLEY. Yes – yes, he's well.

HILDA. That's good. We broke it off six or seven times. It went on for three or four years. I wasn't sure I could live with him.

DUDLEY. No.

HILDA. How is he?

DUDLEY. He'd like to see you.

HILDA. Here?

DUDLEY. Yes.

HILDA. Come here? Oh I don't think that would be a good idea. Anyway, he has to make up his mind, he can't keep dithering between me and Patricia. Poor woman, I do feel for her, and for Stanley of course. He says he's in debt.

DUDLEY. The children are well, I hear.

HILDA. Oh yes, you know I never spend his money, it isn't fair. I have asked Tonks if he could find me some sort of a job, perhaps in a shop, but he says I should paint. He has a high regard for my work. I could perhaps help them, if I could sell, that is. It won't be a happy marriage if they're in debt.

*A* NURSE *enters, wheeling a bed.*

DUDLEY. I'll bring you some books. Do try and rest, Hilda. You must be well, for the children. And for yourself, of course.

HILDA. I've written to Buckingham Palace.

DUDLEY. I beg your pardon.

HILDA. To complain. It can't go on like this, you know.

DUDLEY. I'll . . . I'll come and see you again.

HILDA. Just a minute. (*She bends and rummages in her large, old handbag. She takes out a cheque book, writes a cheque, tears it out and hands it to* DUDLEY.) That's for Stanley. Tell him not to worry.

DUDLEY (*reads the cheque*). Hilda, this is for five thousand pounds!

HILDA. Tell him it's quite all right, I've written to the Palace.

DUDLEY (*baffled*). And you've signed it Mrs. Perkins.

HILDA *nods, smiling.*

## Act Two Scene Nine

HILDA *is in a hospital bed.* STANLEY *goes to her.*

HILDA (*as* STANLEY *gives her a toilet roll*). Stanley, a toilet roll.

STANLEY. Can't get drawing paper on my ration book. It's much warmer down here!

HILDA. But you were able to work in Glasgow . . . (*She lifts the drawings.*)

STANLEY. Oh yes! Dudley thought I wouldn't take to it, but the light! – Oh Hilda. In the early morning . . . mauve skies! Then, down at the shipyards, all pewter and vermilion, just like the blacksmith's at Cookham, only huge.

HILDA. So you got on well.

STANLEY. It rains. Nice people though. One woman asked me if I'd redo her kitchen – me being a painter.

HILDA. Did you?

STANLEY. No. I cried off. In case I made a mess of it.

*They exchange a smile. Silence. A* NURSE *comes in.*

NURSE. Here we are, Mrs. Spencer. (*She puts down a tray of bread and butter and a teacup.*) Only twenty more minutes.

STANLEY. Bread and butter?

*She shakes her head. He gives her tea. She sips. He watches, smiling.*

HILDA. You have some, Stanley.

STANLEY. There's only one cup.

*She gives him her cup of tea. He drinks. Refills the cup, offers it to her, she shakes her head. He drinks.*

HILDA. You look thin. Have you been eating?

STANLEY. Never mind me.

*He eats the bread and butter absently.*

HILDA. I thought they were going to murder us all. I tried to get out of the window. I can't think what came over me, Stanley.

STANLEY. You're better now.

HILDA. Why did I think such things? Whatever made it happen? It's not like me.

STANLEY. God talked to you.

HILDA (*shining eyed*). Yes! Oh Stanley, do you think –

STANLEY. Yes!

HILDA. Making me think things like that?

STANLEY. You were blessed, Hilda. God spoke to you, I'm sure of it.

HILDA (*takes his hand*). I'm so grateful. For everything you've given me. That you want to come and see me. That you love me.

STANLEY. I've got this little cottage now, down the road from where we were. I think about it all the time . . . your coming home. We'll be together.

HILDA. Will we?

STANLEY. I'll make it nice for you. We'll get Elsie back to look after us.

HILDA *turns away. Silence.*

I'm going to get a divorce from Patricia. Then we can get married again – that would be nice, wouldn't it? The girls would be there, everybody . . . if I get the divorce, then everything will be as it was . . . you and me, man and wife, none other, together in the eyes of God, now and always. You'd like that, wouldn't you?

HILDA. Let me get better, Stan. Then I'll think straight. I must have my mind, you see, to be able to think. I get tired, and when I get tired these stupid notions creep in again . . . you say it's God talking to me . . . (*She shakes her head.*)

STANLEY. It's just that he's talking a little more inconveniently. (*He puts his cup down, leans over and kisses her.*) Dear darling Hilda . . . you are my hope . . . I look at you and I am you, oh, you're such a marvellous present to me, and I am so grateful . . . I want to paint an alter-piece of you . . . with all the things we've loved together . . . I want to sit and watch you, I want to stare at you and get it down the way I did, but

I haven't even begun, there's so much of you I haven't
started to get right . . . if I don't get the complexity in the
drawing, how can I hope to tell you . . . speak of you . . .
you're so deep!

*He kisses her hands. She opens her arms and they embrace.*

HILDA. I need some peace, Stanley.

STANLEY. Yes. I know.

NURSE. Mr. Spencer!

STANLEY *falls out of bed. The* NURSE *wheels* HILDA
*apart.* STANLEY *returns to his painting.*

### Act Two Scene Ten

STANLEY *is painting, observed by* HILDA *at a distance.*

STANLEY (*calls*). The foxgloves are out.

You always liked them. Remember that drawing? You
chided me for not putting detail in the leaves and I said,
'I'm being subtle, Hilda'.

I've put up the double bed.

Oh Hilda, you're the absolute essence of joy to me!

*Silence.*

HILDA (*low*). I've been robbed. She stole you from me. She is
a thief.

I had such joy, such ecstasy in you. In the fact that you were
pure. I was the only woman you had ever kissed. I always
felt that you had given me a jewel of great price.

*Silence.*

STANLEY. Please, Hilda. I'm so alone. I'm lonely. It's using
up all my energy.

I keep seeing you, feeling you . . . your hand on the table
with the knuckles all knuckled, and your hair hanging down
like water over smooth stone, and I can come in, and when
you're there I'm with you and I'm with God and it's all
one . . . and everything is All Right! I miss you. I know you

like to be with – quieter people . . . you say when I'm with
you I use up the air . . . but I need you! I've always thought
of you as the most wonderful gift from Heaven, though
you're not in the least like the sort of woman I expected to
fall in love with.

HILDA. Well . . . no matter now. (*As* STANLEY *tries to
answer.*) Too late, Stanley! Oh, why must everything in life
happen out of shape? Just the odd moment of . . . most of the
time, degrees of discord. Why? You've always seen your
way so clearly, but it makes you . . . for happiness between
two people surely there must . . .

You know me. Or you believe you do. You know every line
of me, every cross-hatched surface. Every crevice. But my
mind – ? And I know you . . . every glorious indent of your
countenance . . . your achingly lovely body. No-one knows
you as I do. But I'm not there in your mind. Not in a way
that makes it possible for us to be together.

STANLEY. Is there no basis which would guarantee me from
wanting to bang you on the head!

HILDA. Stanley, please –

STANLEY. You look down all the time . . . you won't look up!
I want our life to be a permanent birthday, I want it to be
love on love!

I want you here. To go about if you must . . . for me the
garden path's far enough, there's so much to do. But only
with you here.

HILDA. I can't come back to Cookham.

STANLEY. Is it because she's here?

You know why I married her. It was social vanity, nothing
more. I was so proud of her. The way she wore clothes,
the way she could talk to people, walk into a room like a
princess.

I had no spiritual relationship with her at all. Ever. I was an
intruder. Eyes colder than a mortuary slab.

HILDA, She took our home and she didn't even live in it.
(*Low.*) I will have nothing – nothing to do with Patricia
Preece. I will not see her, hear her, be in the same room with

her . . . I will not breathe the air she breathes, touch what she has touched. I will not inhabit any space that she has lived in, I will not walk the same streets, nor will I live in the same city, the same land.

And I cannot bear the idea of your divorce from her.

God help me for my meanness, but I find it impossible. Divorce supposes that you have had Patricia for a wife. I cannot bear to have had you touched by her. I want you free of her.

## Act Two Scene Eleven

*The garden at Moor Thatch.* STANLEY *is sitting, his hat in his hands, as* DOROTHY *enters.*

DOROTHY. I'm sorry, Stanley, she won't see you.

STANLEY. That's silly. Why not?

DOROTHY. She says she doesn't see the point.

STANLEY. Well I do!

*Silence.*

Did you – did you put it to her?

DOROTHY. She has your letter.

STANLEY. Did you make it clear – there'd be no problem with the money, she'd be first, top of the list . . . Hilda insists.

DOROTHY *looks in her lap.*

DOROTHY. She is worried about money. (*Looks up with a brief smile.*) It's always a problem, as we both know.

STANLEY. I should be well off by now. As it is, nothing but worry and debt, bills and debt.

DOROTHY. Yes. I'm afraid it's that uncertainty that concerns her.

STANLEY. What's she got to worry about? The courts would be on her side, they were with Hilda.

DOROTHY. She isn't sure what her situation would be. In the case of an annulment.

STANLEY. I'd pay her anyway.

DOROTHY. Yes I'm sure, but – as you say – with two house-
holds . . . your daughters, school fees, doctors' bills . . . how
is Hilda?

STANLEY. Oh, Hilda's fine, absolutely her old self again. I'm
bringing her back.

DOROTHY. Back?

STANLEY. Here. To Cookham.

DOROTHY. To our cottage?

*As* STANLEY *rises, grinning.*

Is she installed?

STANLEY. Not as such.

DOROTHY. I see. (*She rallies.*) I look forward to seeing her,
we've always had such fine talks.

STANLEY. I know. She respects your work, Dorothy.

*Silence.*

Look, try again. I'm not getting anywhere!

DOROTHY. I honestly don't think there's any point. Not for
an annulment. If you were talking of divorce – and – well,
Patricia mentioned the possibility of your settling a sum of
money on her.

STANLEY. How much?

DOROTHY. I couldn't say.

STANLEY. It's all the same in any case. I haven't got any.

PATRICIA *bursts from behind a screen.*

PATRICIA (*to* DOROTHY). You see? And he has the nerve to
turn up here, cap in hand . . . do this . . . do that . . . what
have you got to offer? Look at him! Disgusting! Isn't she
looking after you?

STANLEY. No, I'm on my own.

PATRICIA. Well, let it be understood. There are no favours here. It's for you to maintain me, your legal wife.

STANLEY. Why should I do you any favours? You've had every penny off me, my house – Hilda's house, the house I bought for Hilda and my children – You let that . . . I wasn't allowed in here! I married you because you wanted it, and the minute the ring was on your finger you wouldn't let me through the door. I've looked a complete fool to the whole world, I don't know how I've kept my sanity, and what it did to Hilda is enough to put me in mind of murder.

PATRICIA. Dorothy, please be a witness to that threat.

STANLEY. You have the mouth of a pike, the beak of a cuttlefish, and the eyes of a conger eel.

PATRICIA. Really? Well, you common little man, you'd better take your hat and go, because there are no favours for you here.

STANLEY. I've done you all the favours –

PATRICIA. You? What have you done for me? Did you help me get a show . . . ever? No. You helped neither of us, it's all you, you, you!

STANLEY. If I didn't help you – which is not true, I've tried to mention you . . . if I didn't pull more strings it's because . . . well, why don't you work – you don't work! Dorothy works all the time. When do you work? All you do is spend money and crawl round after that sickly Bloomsbury lot!

PATRICIA. They've been a damned sight more use to me than you have!

STANLEY. Yes, so you suck up to them.

PATRICIA. They happen to be my friends. Civilised people.

STANLEY. Masturbators, you mean.

DOROTHY. Stanley, please!

PATRICIA. What did you say?

STANLEY. They spend more time trying to sell themselves as something special than doing decent work . . . not a single true talent among them, they're either decorators, drunks, or daft in the head.

PATRICIA. I will not listen to you slanging off my friends –

STANLEY. Friends? You don't know the meaning of the word. It's all tit for tat with you, I'll give you this if you give me that . . . I'm wrong, there's no 'giving' about it – you're Trade. I've seen better class in the markets of Macedonia.

PATRICIA. I should like my father to hear you say this.

STANLEY (*laughs*). That's not likely, I've never been allowed near the poor little bugger. You cleaned him out before you started on her . . . (*Points to* DOROTHY.) . . . and then me. I should have seen you coming, Patricia . . . 'Patricia' . . . Ruby, that's your real name . . . good name. What is it about you that makes you think you're some sort of princess, that we must all do your bidding, that we all owe you obedience, and a living, and that you – you have to give Nothing, do nothing . . . just grace us with your presence, and your beauty and your wit . . . not to mention your talent. You are not beautiful enough, you lack wit, you smell like an old fox, and you are sinning against the Holy Spirit when you dare to parade before the world calling yourself an artist. You dampen the word with your stale effluent and wonder why nobody takes you seriously.

PATRICIA. Who are you to talk? People find you funnier than George Robey, you think anyone takes you seriously? Everything you paint is deformed . . . lunatic . . . all gazing out at the world with imbecile stares . . . Me decked out in all the finery you forced upon me . . . Me holding some woman's great big swollen leg! Repulsive creatures everywhere and simple-minded into the bargain. You grabbing at Hilda, begging her to satisfy you, from the bulging great lump between your legs . . . You jumping out of your trousers as some horrible-looking woman rips off her combinations!

STANLEY. Wrong . . . all wrong! You haven't looked! If you'd really looked you might have picked up a thing or two . . . such as How to Paint!

PATRICIA *spits in his face.*

PATRICIA. I suggest – you little guttersnipe – that you begin to take me seriously. You and your hag can do and say what you want. There will be no annulment. And there will be no divorce. I am Mrs Stanley Spencer. You will continue to support me, and you and your Sad Ugly Mistress can learn to live with that, and like it. In the meantime, here are the bills for my framing. I am having a show, thanks to my friends . . . to which your presence will not be welcome.

*She hands the bills to* DOROTHY *who looks at them briefly.*

DOROTHY. Patricia, are you really asking Stanley to pay this?

PATRICIA. You can sort it out between you. Since I'm so ugly and smell so offensively, I'll leave you two graces to see to it.

*Goes.*

DOROTHY. I'm sorry. (*She gives him the bills.*)

STANLEY. You can't honestly be taking her side.

DOROTHY. I must, Stanley. Who else will?

*He looks at her and goes.* PATRICIA *returns.*

PATRICIA. Has he gone?

DOROTHY. Yes.

PATRICIA *sits. And crumples. And cries.* DOROTHY *comforts her.*

DOROTHY. Don't give way to despair, darling.

PATRICIA. That vile Augustus does nothing to help me.

DOROTHY. Nonsense, he's your most ardent patron, your best friend . . . isn't he?

PATRICIA *gives her a scornful look.*

DOROTHY. Patricia, you're not saying –

PATRICIA. I don't want to talk about it.

DOROTHY. You have been adamant with me that despite his reputation, Augustus has never –

PATRICIA. More fool you for believing me! You didn't really suppose that that seedy, suppurant Welshman could cohabit any space without prodding and sucking . . . it's the entry to the milieu – God, I'm sick of myself.

DOROTHY (*numb*). Don't give way.

PATRICIA. What's going to happen to me?

## Act Two Scene Twelve

GWEN *and* STANLEY, *talking quietly. A* NURSE *wheels in* HILDA, *who looks very ill.* GWEN *kisses* HILDA *goodbye, waves to* STANLEY *and goes. The* NURSE *fetches* STANLEY *a chair, smiles and goes.*

STANLEY. Well?

HILDA. They're going to take off my breast.

STANLEY. Oh, ducky! Which one?

HILDA. The left.

STANLEY. Betsy. You'll still have Beatrice. You'll be an Amazon, dearest . . . that's all right, one of a brave and noble race of women.

HILDA. I hated telling you.

STANLEY. It's done now. Don't worry about being frightened. I was frightened when I had my gall bladder out.

HILDA. I know you were.

STANLEY. It rises up in your mouth. It'll be all right, though.

HILDA. Will it?

*They stare at each other, their eyes wide.*

STANLEY. I'll be here.

HILDA. Yes.

**Act Two Scene Thirteen**

HILDA *in bed.* STANLEY *sits at her side. He holds her hand. After a long moment, she turns her head slowly, and smiles at him. He smiles at her. She lies back on the pillow and he sits, very still, holding her hand. Light change.* STANLEY, *in a black overcoat, stands by* HILDA's *bed. The bed is taken away.* STANLEY *gets his pram, sets up his outdoor easel.*

**Act Two Scene Fourteen**

*Promenade (Cookham Village).*

*An* ERRAND BOY *rides past on a bicycle with a large basket. An* ELDERLY MAN *crosses with his dog.* STANLEY *whistling Mozart.* MRS BELLAMY, *with a shopping basket, crosses.*

STANLEY. 'Morning, Mrs. Bellamy.

*But* MRS. BELLAMY *can only giggle at him and hurry off. A* WORKMAN *goes by.*

WORKMAN. Morning Mr. Spencer . . . oh . . . got that wrong, an't I? Be Lord Spencer now, eh?

STANLEY. No. Sir Stanley.

*The* WORKMAN *stares at* STANLEY *reverently.*

WORKMAN; My word.

STANLEY. I still fart, you know.

*The* WORKMAN *goes off, laughing.* STANLEY *sits on his little stool.*

STANLEY. I cooked myself a proper breakfast this morning, ducky. And washed up. I wanted to feel all virtuous and ready. (*Lifts his face to the sun, closing his eyes.*) Sun's coming. I shall be able to do the shadows.

ELSIE. Morning Stan.

STANLEY. Morning Elsie.

ELSIE. Not working then?

STANLEY. I'm waiting for the light on that puddle so's I can begin where I left off yesterday.

ELSIE. We're ever so pleased, all of us. Puts Cookham on the map, eh? Sir Stanley!

*She giggles.* STANLEY *joins in.*

STANLEY. I know! Still.

ELSIE. Still.

*They savour the moment.*

ELSIE. I must get on, I got to cut some greens for his dinner.

STANLEY (*watching her go*). Never did get her buttocks right. What I need . . . I need a good English wind to blow away all that cloud. I want a clear sky and a good Boudin blue . . . a good mix of blues . . . Then I'll knock it down with tone. Ah! The sun! (*As the sun comes out, the* VICAR *rides by.*)

VICAR. Congratulations, Stanley! (*Sees* DOROTHY *and* PATRICIA.) Good morning Miss Hepworth, Mrs Spencer.

*Two* BOYS *arrive and watch* STANLEY *work.*

PATRICIA. Lady Spencer, if you would.

VICAR (*getting to his feet*). Oh . . . doesn't that have to wait for the investiture?

DOROTHY *herds the indignant* PATRICIA *away.*

PATRICIA. Common little man – the jealousy! Well, they're all going to have to bend the knee to me now!

*The boys,* BRIAN *and* TIM, *lean close.*

BRIAN. Why are the people all funny shapes?

ELSIE, *returning with her greens, crosses.* STANLEY *looks across at her. The* BOYS *laugh.* SUMMERS, *a reporter, accosts* DOROTHY *and* PATRICIA *after the* VICAR *points them out.*

SUMMERS. Lady Spencer? Beg your pardon – wondered if I might have a few words.

PATRICIA. *The Times?*

SUMMERS. *News Chronicle.* Congratulations on your elevation. Much deserved, if I may say.

BRIAN. We got a painting of Jesus at school.

TIM. With a lamp in his hand.

BRIAN. Outside the privy.

STANLEY. Think I might have seen that one.

BRIAN. Yours are good, though.

> *They watch* STANLEY *work.*

> Who else is good?

STANLEY. We-ell . . . I'm best of course. Then there's . . . Signorelli . . . Pintoricchio . . . Uccello . . . Piero della Francesca . . . Fra Angelico . . . Giotto of course . . .

BRIAN (*nods knowledgably*). Oh ah.

TIM. Caw.

> PATRICIA *and* DOROTHY *are sitting on a park seat with* SUMMERS.

SUMMERS. Was it a surprise, the knighthood, ladies?

> PATRICIA *and* DOROTHY *exchange a look.* DOROTHY *makes to speak.*

PATRICIA (*quickly*). Not at all, we were expecting it.

SUMMERS. Could I ask Sir Stanley's reaction?

> *As they do not reply.*

> I believe he's from . . . ah . . . quite an ordinary background . . . I mean, before he became so well-known.

PATRICIA. This is Miss Hepworth – Dorothy Hepworth. She paints – we are both painters of repute – you might make a note of that.

SUMMERS. I believe you and Sir Stanley are no longer living together?

> PATRICIA *glares at him.*

DOROTHY. Sir Stanley needs a good deal of solitude for his work.

SUMMERS. I mean as man and wife.

DOROTHY. I don't think we need go any further with this.

SUMMERS. Sorry, didn't mean to intrude . . . (*Follows them.*) . . . if I could just have a few words aboout Sir Stanley's work –

PATRICIA (*turns on him*). Most of Stanley Spencer's work, in my opinion – and I was trained at the Slade – is either vulgar or deranged. Good-day.

*She sweeps off.*

SUMMERS. Miss Hepworth?

DOROTHY. I –

SUMMERS. Yes?

DOROTHY. I'd like to say that Sir Stanley Spencer is rightly acclaimed as one of England's greatest painters. I believe him to be uniquely gifted. He has a . . . how shall I say . . . there is a sort of unique human clumsiness about his work – it's deliberate, of course. He paints people trapped, as it were, in their own flesh, pinned down to this earth, and yet they seek to soar and he makes that seem so very possible. You will have to look very hard to find a better draughts-man – Vermeer perhaps. For invention he has no peer . . . and everything is celebrated and revered with a balance that speaks of the most tender spiritual equality. He honours the smallest detail. I particularly draw your attention to Sir Stanley's colours . . . without the shout of a colourist, they nonetheless show the most infinite variety of subtlety and tone. Very English.

SUMMERS. Thank you, Miss Hepworth.

DOROTHY. Good morning.

TIM. What sort of tree is that?

STANLEY. Beech. You can tell by the bark – smooth.

TIM. We got a big privet bush in our garden.

STANLEY. I know it. Nice flowers.

TIM. Yeah. Do smell though.

BRIAN. Cat's piss.

STANLEY (*abstracted, working*). Mmm, a bit.

TIM. Come on, our Brian. 'Bye, Mr Spencer.

BRIAN. So long.

STANLEY (*busy*). 'Bye.

> The VICAR *goes by again. And then* HILDA *appears. She stands behind* STANLEY, *watching him quietly. And then she goes.* STANLEY *works. A retired* COLONEL, *with his wife, approaches.*

COLONEL. Morning.

> STANLEY *nods, smiles.*

Congratulations, Spencer.

WIFE. Our very best wishes to you. You will come to dinner?

> STANLEY *peers up at her, surprised.*

STANLEY. Thanks. Perhaps.

> *He works. The* COLONEL *watches, his* WIFE *seeks to draw him away.*

COLONEL. Funny angle, that.

STANLEY. It's the short perspective.

COLONEL. What?

STANLEY. I'm seeing things a bit from above, doncha know. The way God would see them. You're looking down. With love.

COLONEL. Oh. Ah. I see.

> *He and his* WIFE *go.* MRS. BELLAMY *returns in a hurry, giggles as she passes* STANLEY. *Alone,* STANLEY *works, humming.*

STANLEY (*sings*). 'Improve thy knowledge with due care, In all thy life thyself prepare' . . .

Remember when I came down to Devon that time? After you'd been ill? And they wouldn't let me stay with you, so I slept in a beach hut, and you said the sea was like opals?

This is for your altar piece. I'm really trying to hang on to it – simplicity – not like something separate on a shelf but in me . . . real, alive. Then I can do you properly. Oh I wish I could smell you . . . that buttery smell of your hair . . . your body smelling of cobnuts. I keep the cupboard shut on your clothes so it won't go away, the smell. I pick up your shoes. I use your comb. I've even got your flannel.

Oh ducky, I feel so close to you. You're in me – you-and-me. The only being I can talk to, that I've ever wanted to talk to. It's so wonderful talking to you, and never having to be careful of what I say, or whether you won't understand – I feel you understand everything now. That you're looking out for me. It makes me feel closer to Heaven with you there. Specially after work, when I'm tired. I see this great picture of God and all His Angels sitting on these beautiful three-dimensional clouds and on His left hand sits Bach and on His right hand Stanley! I'm only joking of course.

You'll love this when it's done. I'm going to do Christ glorying in His gorgeousness, I want him in a great, gallivanting, lying-down sprawl on the greensward. Rather far from Holy Writ I daresay, but I don't know why they think what I'm doing is pagan, what am I supposed to paint? I don't know the flowers around Galilee, the flowers I know are buttercups and daisies. It's no good doing palm trees – I'm English, so I do the Englishness of things. You do the things you love. For His glory.

You know what I think, Hilda? I think an artist is the mediator between God and man. He could even be next in divinity to the saint. Like the saint her performs miracles. With God's help of course. God's at his elbow, telling him what to rub out.

*Pause.*

You didn't look after yourself, you know. You should have done, for me and the girls. You should have thought about yourself more, made sure you were happy. Then you wouldn't have been so ill and we wouldn't have to . . .

*He can't go on. He takes a moment to recover himself.*

I'm not lonely. I loved being with you, but I enjoy it here on my own. You're here in my imagination. In some ways it's better. I make up your answers for you and sometimes they – well, sometimes they suit me better. I hope you don't mind. People often ask me if I'm lonely. I say no, I'm not lonely. I've had a great love, do you see? I've been blessed. God blessed me with a talent and a great love. Now I'm alone to get on with the work. Sorrow and sadness is not me.

*He gets up, straightens, looks down at the canvas.*

Beautifully done.

*He packs up his things, puts them on the pram. And goes.*